GRADUATING

FROM

POVERTY

By

Lalit Mohanty

PREFACE

The world has long believed in the power of education to change lives. We are taught from a young age that academic success will lead to a stable job, a comfortable life, and eventually, financial security. Yet, despite this widely accepted belief, many highly educated individuals find themselves struggling financially, caught in a cycle of working for money rather than having money work for them.

This book, **Graduating from Poverty: The Financial Education School Forgot**, aims to shed light on a simple but often overlooked truth: traditional education alone is not enough to make you rich. While schooling prepares us for jobs, it rarely teaches us how to build wealth, manage money, or create financial independence. Instead, it promotes a mindset centered around job security and earning wages— one that leaves many trapped in the rat race, unaware of the opportunities that lie outside the academic sphere.

I wrote this book because I've seen first-hand how following the conventional path of education leads many to financial struggle, while those who break free from this path and embrace financial literacy, entrepreneurship, and investing find themselves on the road to wealth. I have spent years studying the habits of the wealthy and comparing them with the financial behaviors instilled through traditional education. The patterns are clear: those who acquire the right financial knowledge and embrace a mindset of growth and risk-taking are the ones who achieve financial freedom.

In this book, I will guide you through the limitations of the traditional education system, what it fails to teach about money, and, most importantly, how you can fill those gaps. Whether you're a student, a working professional, or someone simply looking to escape the middle-class trap, this book will offer you the insights and tools you need to achieve financial independence.

The goal is not to dismiss the value of education but to recognize its limitations. To truly succeed in today's world, you need to go beyond the classroom and acquire the knowledge that traditional schooling often overlooks: financial literacy, investing, entrepreneurship, and the mindset that prioritizes long-term wealth over immediate gratification.

I hope this book inspires you to take control of your financial future, to challenge the norms of traditional education, and to create a life where money becomes a tool for freedom rather than a source of stress.

Welcome to a journey of financial transformation.

— Lalit Prasad Mohanty

TABLE OF CONTENTS

Introduction: The Education Illusion

- The False Promise of Traditional Education
- Why Academic Success Doesn't Guarantee Financial Success
- Understanding the Disconnect Between Schooling and Wealth

Part I: The Problem – Why Traditional Education Keeps You Poor

Chapter 1: The Education Trap – A Job-Oriented Mindset

- The Focus on Job Security and Climbing the Corporate Ladder
- How Traditional Education Conditions You to Be a Worker, Not a Wealth Creator

Chapter 2: What Schools Don't Teach About Money

- The Lack of Financial Literacy in the Curriculum

- Understanding Income, Debt, and Basic Financial Concepts Schools Miss

Chapter 3: The Dangers of Relying Solely on Salaries

- Why Relying on One Source of Income is Risky
- How Salaries Limit Your Wealth Potential

Part II: The Solution – Gaining the Right Financial Knowledge

Chapter 4: Financial Literacy – The Essential Knowledge to Build Wealth

- The Key Areas of Financial Literacy: Budgeting, Saving, Debt, and Investing
- Understanding How Money Works to Achieve Financial Freedom

Chapter 5: Developing the Entrepreneurial and Investor Mindset

- Shifting from an Employee to an Entrepreneur and Investor Mentality
- How to Embrace Risk, Innovation, and Opportunity for Wealth Creation

Chapter 6: Building Multiple Income Streams

- The Power of Passive Income: Real Estate, Stocks, and Businesses
- Diversifying Income to Maximize Wealth and Reduce Financial Risk

Chapter 7: Leveraging Technology for Financial Growth

- How the Internet and Global Markets Provide Wealth-Building Opportunities

- Using Online Resources to Gain Knowledge and Create Wealth

Part III: Examples – Success Stories and Case Studies

Chapter 8: Case Studies of Financial Transformation

- How Individuals Broke Free from the Education Trap and Built Wealth

- Stories of People Who Became Rich by Embracing Financial Literacy, Entrepreneurship, and Investment

Chapter 9: From Corporate Employee to Financial Freedom

- Real-Life Examples of People Who Shifted from a Job-Oriented Life to Building Passive Income Streams

Chapter 10: The Self-Education Path to Wealth

- How Self-Education in Financial Literacy and Investing Created Wealth for Non-Traditional Learners

Part IV: Conclusion – Taking Control of Your Financial Future

Chapter 11: Practical Steps to Escape the Education Trap

- Conducting a Personal Financial Health Check

- The Action Plan for Acquiring Financial Knowledge and Creating Wealth

Chapter 12: The Role of Mindset in Sustaining Wealth

- Prioritizing Long-Term Wealth Over Short-Term Gratification

- The Ongoing Commitment to Financial Growth and Independence

Chapter 13: The Future of Education and Wealth Creation

- Why Financial Literacy and Entrepreneurship Must Be Part of Modern Education

- Creating Your Own Path to Financial Freedom

INTRODUCTION

THE EDUCATION ILLUSION

1. Introduction to Self-Education and Its Importance

In an age where information is more accessible than ever, self-education has emerged as a critical tool for personal and financial growth. Self-education can be defined as the process of learning and acquiring knowledge independently, outside the confines of traditional educational institutions. This approach to learning enables individuals to take control of their education, tailoring it to their interests, goals, and specific needs.

While formal education provides foundational knowledge and skills, it often lacks the practical insights necessary for real-world financial success. Traditional schools and universities typically emphasize theoretical concepts and standardized curricula, focusing on preparing students for employment rather than fostering financial independence or entrepreneurial thinking. As a result, many graduates find themselves ill-equipped to navigate the complexities of personal finance, investing, and wealth-building.

Self-education fills this gap by allowing individuals to pursue knowledge in a way that aligns with their unique circumstances and aspirations. It empowers learners to delve into topics that are often overlooked in conventional education, such as financial literacy, investment strategies, entrepreneurship, and personal development. By actively seeking out information through books, online courses, podcasts, and other resources, self-educators can cultivate a deeper understanding of how money works and how to leverage it to create wealth.

The importance of self-education cannot be overstated, especially in today's fast-paced and ever-changing economic landscape. With advancements in technology, the rise of the gig economy, and the increasing complexity of financial markets, the ability to learn independently has become essential for achieving financial independence. Self-education fosters critical thinking, adaptability, and a growth mindset—traits that are crucial for overcoming challenges and seizing opportunities in both personal and professional realms.

Moreover, self-education allows individuals to take ownership of their learning journey, enabling them to set their own pace and explore topics that resonate with their interests and passions. This personalized approach not only makes learning more engaging but also encourages a lifelong commitment to growth and improvement.

Why Academic Success Doesn't Guarantee Financial Success

For decades, society has championed academic success as the primary pathway to a prosperous life. Graduating with high honors from prestigious universities is often equated with future financial stability and career advancement. However, the reality is far more nuanced. Despite the credentials and accolades that accompany academic achievement, many individuals find themselves struggling financially, trapped in a cycle of debt, or unable to achieve their desired lifestyle. Understanding why academic success does not automatically translate to financial success is crucial for anyone seeking to break free from the traditional education trap.

1. The Narrow Focus of Traditional Education

Traditional education is designed to impart knowledge and skills primarily relevant to the workforce. While this is essential for preparing students for specific careers, it often overlooks critical aspects of financial literacy and personal finance management. Courses on budgeting, investing, debt management, and entrepreneurship are frequently absent from standard curricula. As a result, even the brightest students may graduate without the practical knowledge needed to manage their finances effectively.

Many students leave school equipped with theoretical knowledge but lacking the tools to navigate real-world financial challenges. They may excel in subjects like mathematics or science but struggle to apply that knowledge to everyday financial decisions. This disconnect can lead to poor financial habits, such as excessive spending, inadequate savings, and a lack of investment knowledge, ultimately hindering their financial success.

2. The Debt Dilemma

In pursuit of higher education, many students accumulate substantial debt in the form of student loans. The average student loan debt in many countries can be staggering, often exceeding tens of thousands of dollars. Graduating with such a burden can create significant financial pressure, making it challenging to establish a solid financial foundation.

The expectation that a degree will automatically lead to a high-paying job can exacerbate this issue. Many graduates enter the job market only to find that the roles available to them do not pay enough to cover their living expenses, let alone their debt repayments. This scenario creates a cycle where graduates are forced to prioritize immediate financial obligations over long-term wealth-building strategies.

3. The Job Market is Evolving

The modern job market is dynamic and often unpredictable. Rapid technological advancements and shifting economic landscapes mean that many traditional career paths are no longer as stable or lucrative as they once were. Fields that were once considered secure can become obsolete overnight, leaving graduates scrambling to adapt.

Moreover, the rise of automation and artificial intelligence has transformed the workforce, with many entry-level jobs disappearing or evolving beyond recognition. Academic success may provide a solid foundation for entering a profession, but it does not guarantee job security or advancement in an ever-changing landscape. Individuals who lack the skills to adapt or pivot in response to market demands may find themselves at a disadvantage.

4. Entrepreneurial Skills and Mindset

While academic achievement emphasizes critical thinking and problem-solving, it often falls short in fostering an entrepreneurial mindset. The ability to identify opportunities, take calculated risks, and innovate is crucial for financial success, yet these skills are rarely prioritized in traditional education.

Many successful entrepreneurs and investors are self-taught individuals who have gained knowledge and experience outside the confines of formal education. They understand that wealth creation often involves creativity, resilience, and a willingness to learn from failure. Academic success alone does not cultivate these traits, which are essential for thriving in today's economy.

5. The Importance of Networking and Relationships

Financial success is not solely about knowledge; it is also about relationships. Many opportunities arise from networking, mentorship, and collaboration. While academic environments do provide some networking opportunities, they often focus on connecting with peers within a specific field rather than cultivating broader relationships that can lead to diverse opportunities.

Successful individuals often credit their financial success to the connections they made outside of formal education, whether through internships, industry events, or entrepreneurial endeavors. Academic success may provide a strong foundation, but it is the ability to forge meaningful relationships that can open doors to new opportunities and financial growth.

6. A Different Definition of Success

Finally, the conventional definition of success often equates it with a high-paying job and financial security. However, this perspective can be limiting and may not resonate with everyone. Many people find fulfillment and financial success through unconventional paths, such as starting their own businesses or pursuing freelance work. These avenues often require skills and knowledge that are not typically taught in schools.

By narrowing the definition of success to academic achievement, society overlooks the diverse ways individuals can create wealth and achieve financial independence. Self-education, entrepreneurship, and alternative career paths can lead to financial success in ways that traditional education cannot.

Understanding the Disconnect Between Schooling and Wealth

In contemporary society, there exists a widely held belief that a formal education is the most reliable pathway to financial success. This belief is deeply ingrained in cultural narratives, family expectations, and societal structures. However, the reality is that there is often a significant disconnect between the knowledge and skills acquired through formal schooling and the practical financial acumen required to build and sustain wealth. Understanding this disconnect is crucial for individuals seeking to navigate their financial futures effectively.

1. The Curriculum Gap

One of the most glaring issues in traditional education is the lack of practical financial literacy within the curriculum. Most educational systems prioritize subjects such as mathematics, science, history, and literature, while neglecting essential topics like personal finance, investing, and entrepreneurship.

Students may excel academically but leave school without a fundamental understanding of how to manage their money, create budgets, or invest wisely.

This gap in education is particularly concerning given that financial decisions play a crucial role in determining an individual's quality of life. Without the tools to make informed financial choices, graduates may struggle with debt management, investment strategies, and overall financial planning, ultimately hindering their ability to accumulate wealth.

2. Overemphasis on Standardized Testing

Traditional education systems often place a heavy emphasis on standardized testing, which measures a student's ability to memorize and regurgitate information rather than their capacity to think critically or apply knowledge to real-world situations. This focus on test performance can lead to a superficial understanding of subjects and neglect the development of practical skills necessary for financial success.

Students may graduate with high grades yet lack the practical experience or knowledge to navigate financial challenges. The ability to excel in an exam does not equate to the ability to manage personal finances, invest in the stock market, or start a business. This misalignment creates a disconnect between academic success and real-world financial acumen.

3. Lack of Real-World Experience

Another factor contributing to the disconnect between schooling and wealth is the limited exposure to real-world financial scenarios within the educational environment. Most formal education systems do not provide students with hands-on experience in managing finances, investing, or running a business. Instead, students are often confined to theoretical discussions without the opportunity to apply their knowledge in practical settings.

Internships, apprenticeships, and experiential learning opportunities are often scarce in traditional schooling. As a result, students may graduate without ever having faced the financial realities of budgeting, saving, or investing. This lack of practical experience can lead to a steep learning curve once they enter the workforce, as they must navigate these challenges without prior exposure or preparation.

4. The Impact of Socioeconomic Background

Socioeconomic status plays a significant role in shaping an individual's financial literacy and opportunities for wealth creation. Students from lower-income backgrounds often lack access to financial education resources, mentorship, and networks that could help them build wealth. While wealthier families may provide their children with exposure to financial literacy through discussions, resources, and opportunities, those from disadvantaged backgrounds may find themselves at a disadvantage.

This disparity creates a cycle of financial illiteracy and limited opportunities. Without access to the knowledge and resources necessary to make informed financial decisions, individuals from lower socioeconomic backgrounds may struggle to break free from poverty, perpetuating the cycle of financial hardship.

5. The Illusion of Job Security

Many traditional educational narratives promote the idea that obtaining a degree will lead to stable employment and financial security. However, the reality is that job security has become increasingly elusive in today's economy. Rapid technological advancements, globalization, and changing market demands have resulted in the obsolescence of many traditional jobs, leaving graduates vulnerable to unemployment and underemployment.

This illusion of job security can lead individuals to overlook the importance of entrepreneurship, investing, and alternative income streams. Graduates may focus solely on securing a "good job" rather than exploring opportunities for wealth creation outside the confines of traditional employment.

6. Cultural Attitudes Toward Money

Cultural attitudes toward money and financial success also play a significant role in the disconnect between schooling and wealth. In many cultures, discussions about money are often considered taboo, leading to a lack of open dialogue about financial literacy, budgeting, and investing. This silence perpetuates misconceptions about money and limits individuals' understanding of how to build wealth.

Furthermore, societal narratives that equate success with academic achievement can overshadow the importance of financial literacy. Individuals may feel pressured to pursue degrees and conventional career paths, believing that academic success alone will lead to financial security. This narrow perspective can hinder their ability to explore alternative routes to wealth creation, such as entrepreneurship or investing.

7. The Need for Holistic Education

To bridge the gap between schooling and wealth, there is an urgent need for a more holistic approach to education that prioritizes practical financial literacy alongside traditional academic subjects. Incorporating financial education into the curriculum, offering experiential learning opportunities, and fostering discussions about money can equip students with the knowledge and skills needed to navigate their financial futures.

Educational institutions must recognize that preparing students for the real world involves more than just academic excellence; it requires instilling practical financial skills, promoting entrepreneurial thinking, and encouraging a proactive approach to wealth creation.

Conclusion

Understanding the disconnect between schooling and wealth is essential for individuals seeking to achieve financial independence. While academic success is undoubtedly valuable, it must be complemented by practical financial knowledge and skills. By recognizing the limitations of traditional education and taking charge of their financial education, individuals can empower themselves to make informed financial decisions, pursue wealth-building opportunities, and ultimately break free from the constraints of conventional educational narratives. In doing so, they can forge their own paths to financial success, regardless of their academic achievements.

CHAPTER 1

THE EDUCATION TRAP – A JOB-ORIENTED MINDSET

The Focus on Job Security and Climbing the Corporate Ladder

From an early age, traditional education instills in us a singular goal: to secure a stable job. The promise of job security becomes the ultimate reward for completing a structured path—good grades, a degree, and finally, a well-paying position in a reputable organization. This trajectory seems to offer a sense of safety, but it comes at a cost that few recognize. Instead of fostering innovation, critical thinking, or entrepreneurship, traditional education channels individuals into a job-oriented mindset, focusing on security rather than opportunity.

The Safety Net Illusion

The lure of job security is deeply embedded in societal norms. For many middle-class families, stability is the pinnacle of success. Parents, schools, and institutions emphasize getting a "safe" job over any other pursuit. This mindset, however, traps individuals into believing that once they secure a job, they've reached the finish line. The truth is, this job-oriented thinking limits long-term financial growth and independence. The illusion of safety comes from the comfort of a paycheck, but as soon as the paycheck stops, whether through layoffs or retirement, the foundation crumbles.

Climbing the Corporate Ladder – A Slow, Risky Journey

The corporate ladder promises rewards for those who diligently climb it. Promotions, bonuses, and the potential for higher salaries lure individuals into dedicating years to a singular career path. However, this system is inherently limited. For one, it forces people to trade time for money, locking them into a linear progression where financial gains are slow and depend entirely on the organization's willingness to promote them.

Moreover, climbing the corporate ladder involves navigating office politics, dealing with bureaucracy, and adjusting to constant shifts in the corporate landscape. Companies may merge, restructure, or downsize, leaving employees vulnerable despite years of loyalty. The ladder is steep, and many spend decades striving for the top, only to realize that their efforts have capped their income potential and that they are heavily dependent on an employer for their financial well-being.

The Problem with Job-Oriented Education

Traditional education does not teach wealth creation or financial independence. It trains students to be good employees, not employers or investors. Schools focus on rote learning, preparing students for exams and interviews but offering little to no education on personal finance, investing, or entrepreneurship. The emphasis on obtaining a job overlooks the importance of building multiple income streams or understanding how wealth truly grows.

Financial literacy is glaringly absent from most curricula, leaving students unequipped to manage money or grow wealth effectively. This gap in knowledge traps individuals in a cycle of dependence, where they rely on an employer for financial security rather than creating their own financial freedom. Without an understanding of how to leverage investments or passive income, many remain stuck in the mindset that working harder or getting promoted is the only way to improve their financial situation.

How Traditional Education Keeps You Poor

The job-oriented mindset fails to acknowledge the fundamental differences between earning a wage and building wealth. Most people, guided by traditional education, spend their entire lives working for money rather than having money work for them. This is where the trap lies: by prioritizing a stable job over entrepreneurial or investment opportunities, people miss out on the powerful wealth-building potential that comes from understanding the power of compounding, passive income, and financial risk-taking.

Even for those who manage to climb the corporate ladder, wealth is often limited by salary caps, taxes, and inflation. Promotions or pay raises may offer a temporary sense of financial relief, but they are often accompanied by increased responsibility and workload, which may lead to burnout. More importantly, relying solely on a job means that financial security is at the mercy of the employer, industry trends, or even global economic conditions—factors entirely outside of an individual's control.

Breaking Free from the Education Trap

To break free from this trap, it's crucial to adopt a new mindset—one that prioritizes financial independence over job security. This shift starts with understanding that wealth creation doesn't come from working for others but from investing in yourself, your skills, and opportunities that generate passive income. By exploring entrepreneurship, investing, and other avenues for building wealth, individuals can move away from the limitations of traditional education and job-centric thinking.

Ultimately, climbing the corporate ladder is not inherently wrong. It works for some, but it should not be the only path to success. Traditional education's fixation on job security creates a false sense of accomplishment, leading people to overlook the vast potential of creating financial freedom outside of a job. To escape the middle-class trap, individuals must realize that there is more to financial success than a paycheck—there's ownership, investment, and the ability to make money work for you, rather than the other way around.

How Traditional Education Conditions You to Be a Worker, Not a Wealth Creator

Traditional education, as it stands, is designed to produce workers who can fit into the existing economic framework. The school system, from primary education to university, is structured in a way that promotes conformity, discipline, and a mindset geared toward employment rather than entrepreneurship or wealth creation. The focus on standardized tests, rigid curricula, and the memorization of information subtly conditions individuals to think like workers, not wealth creators. This chapter explores how education shapes this mindset and how breaking free from it is essential for those who seek financial independence.

The History of Education: A System for Workers

To understand how traditional education conditions individuals to be workers, it's important to examine the roots of modern schooling. The current education system emerged during the Industrial Revolution when societies needed skilled workers to fill factories and bureaucratic offices. Schools were designed to teach obedience, punctuality, and repetitive tasks—skills required in factories and corporate environments. This system worked well for industrialized economies, but it fell short in cultivating creativity, entrepreneurship, or independent thinking.

The traditional classroom mimics the structure of a factory, with a teacher at the front directing students, much like a manager instructing workers. Students are expected to follow instructions, complete assignments, and meet deadlines, reinforcing the idea that success comes from complying with authority and adhering to preset guidelines. This framework discourages questioning the status quo or seeking alternative paths—two traits essential for wealth creation.

The Focus on Employment, Not Ownership

Traditional education reinforces the belief that the ultimate goal of learning is to secure a job. Throughout school, students are told that good grades lead to good colleges, which, in turn, lead to good jobs. The entire system orients individuals toward employment as the only viable means of financial success. Owning a business, becoming an investor, or pursuing other wealth-building opportunities are rarely discussed, let alone encouraged.

The curriculum itself is tailored toward creating employees. Most courses emphasize specialized knowledge in a particular field—be it engineering, medicine, law, or business administration—so students can fit neatly into the labor force. While these fields can be lucrative, they still condition students to think in terms of selling their time and skills to someone else, not creating wealth on their own terms.

Schools rarely teach the skills required to become an owner or an investor. Concepts like managing cash flow, leveraging debt to build wealth, or the power of compounding investments are almost entirely absent. Instead, the emphasis is on preparing for a stable job, securing a paycheck, and climbing a hierarchical structure where wealth is often capped by salary limits.

The Absence of Financial Education

One of the most glaring shortcomings of traditional education is the near-total absence of financial literacy. Students graduate with knowledge in their chosen fields but lack even a basic understanding of how to manage money, let alone grow it. Schools don't teach how to invest in stocks, real estate, or businesses, nor do they cover essential topics like taxes, inflation, or the power of passive income. Without this foundation, individuals are left to navigate the complexities of personal finance on their own, often making costly mistakes along the way.

This lack of financial education perpetuates the worker mindset because it keeps people reliant on their jobs as their primary or only source of income. Without the tools to create multiple income streams or invest in wealth-generating assets, most people believe their financial well-being depends solely on earning more from their employers. This dependency on a paycheck limits the potential for financial freedom and wealth creation.

The Risk-Averse Mentality

Traditional education also conditions people to be risk-averse, a key trait of a worker mindset. In school, mistakes are penalized, and students are taught that failure is something to be avoided at all costs. This fear of failure carries over into adulthood, where people avoid risks that could potentially lead to greater rewards—such as starting a business or making investments—because they've been conditioned to seek security over opportunity.

Wealth creation, however, often involves taking calculated risks. Entrepreneurs, investors, and wealth creators know that failure is part of the learning process. They understand that to grow, one must be willing to step outside of their comfort zone and take chances. Traditional education does not promote this mindset. Instead, it teaches students to follow a safe, linear path, which typically leads to a stable job but not necessarily to financial independence.

The Trade of Time for Money

One of the most fundamental ways traditional education conditions individuals to be workers is by promoting the idea that success is achieved by trading time for money. In schools, students learn that the more effort they put in (in the form of studying or completing assignments), the better their results (grades) will be. This one-to-one correlation between effort and reward is ingrained in the educational process and mirrors the employment model, where workers trade their time for wages or salaries.

However, true wealth creation comes from breaking this connection between time and money. Wealthy individuals understand that in order to scale their income, they need to move beyond working for money and make their money work for them. This could be through investing in assets that generate passive income, owning a business that can grow without direct involvement, or other strategies that decouple income from time. Traditional education rarely, if ever, touches on these concepts, leaving most individuals stuck in the paradigm of trading time for money, with limited prospects for financial growth.

Conformity over Creativity

Finally, traditional education values conformity over creativity. Students are rewarded for giving the "right" answers and penalized for thinking outside the box. This stifles the creative and entrepreneurial spirit, which is essential for wealth creation. Innovation, after all, comes from challenging norms, thinking differently, and creating solutions where others see problems.

Entrepreneurs and investors thrive on creative thinking. They are constantly seeking new opportunities, developing innovative products or services, and finding ways to disrupt industries. Traditional education, with its focus on memorization and repetition, suppresses these skills, conditioning individuals to follow established paths rather than forge their own.

Breaking Free: Becoming a Wealth Creator

To transition from a worker to a wealth creator, one must first break free from the conditioning of traditional education. This shift begins by recognizing that the job-oriented mindset instilled by schooling is not the only path to financial success.

True wealth comes from ownership, investment, and understanding how to make money work for you, not the other way around.

Education needs to go beyond just preparing individuals for employment. It should equip them with the tools to create, invest, and build wealth. This means seeking out financial literacy, learning about investments, and understanding how to take calculated risks. By embracing a mindset focused on wealth creation, rather than job security, individuals can unlock their potential to achieve financial independence and build lasting wealth.

CHAPTER 2

WHAT SCHOOLS DON'T TEACH ABOUT MONEY

The Lack of Financial Literacy in the Curriculum

In most school systems worldwide, students are taught a wide array of subjects ranging from mathematics, science, history, and literature. While these subjects are essential for developing critical thinking, creativity, and basic life skills, a glaring gap exists in the curriculum: financial literacy. Understanding how money works, how to manage it effectively, and how to make it grow through investments is crucial for success in the real world, yet these topics are rarely addressed in formal education. This chapter explores why financial literacy is missing from schools, the impact of this gap on individuals, and how this omission perpetuates the cycle of poverty and middle-class stagnation.

2.1 The Overemphasis on Academic Knowledge

Schools are designed to prepare students for the workforce, but the focus is often on academic achievement rather than practical, everyday skills. Students are encouraged to excel in standardized tests, memorize formulas, and write essays on historical events, but they are not taught how to budget, save, or invest their earnings. This lack of real-world financial education leaves students vulnerable when they enter adulthood. They graduate with diplomas, degrees, and theoretical knowledge but are ill-equipped to handle the financial decisions that come with earning a living.

One of the reasons for this overemphasis on academic knowledge is that traditional education systems were developed during the Industrial Revolution. At that time, schools were designed to create a workforce that could follow instructions, perform repetitive tasks, and contribute to an industrialized economy. The world has changed since then, but the educational model remains largely the same. Instead of adapting to the needs of a rapidly evolving global economy, schools continue to churn out students who are trained to be employees rather than financially independent individuals.

2.2 The Cost of Financial Ignorance

The lack of financial education in schools has far-reaching consequences. Many young adults leave school and enter the workforce with little understanding of basic financial principles such as budgeting, credit, taxes, and retirement planning. As a result, they often fall into debt, live paycheck to paycheck, and struggle to build any significant wealth. Without the tools to manage money effectively, they are more likely to take on high-interest loans, max out credit cards, and fail to invest for their future.

Financial ignorance can also lead to poor decisions when it comes to major life milestones like buying a home, starting a business, or saving for retirement. Many middle-class individuals believe that buying a house is always a good investment, without fully understanding the costs involved, the risks of taking on too much debt, or the potential for economic downturns that could impact property values. Similarly, they may contribute to a pension plan or a savings account without understanding how inflation erodes their savings over time, or how compound interest could significantly boost their wealth if invested wisely.

2.3 Why Schools Don't Teach Financial Literacy

One might wonder why such an important subject is not prioritized in the educational system. There are several reasons for this, each revealing deeper systemic issues.

2.3.1 Outdated Educational Models

As mentioned earlier, the traditional education system was designed to prepare students for a job-oriented economy, not one in which financial independence or entrepreneurship is the goal. The focus has been on teaching skills that employers demand rather than skills that foster self-reliance and financial growth. This outdated model continues to influence curriculum decisions, leaving financial literacy on the sidelines.

2.3.2 Lack of Qualified Teachers

Teaching financial literacy requires educators who are well-versed in personal finance, investing, and economics. Unfortunately, many teachers themselves lack this knowledge because they, too, have been through the same education system that neglected financial literacy. Without proper training or resources, teachers may feel ill-equipped to instruct students on topics they are not familiar with, further perpetuating the problem.

2.3.3 Financial Education Isn't Seen as a Priority

In many countries, education policymakers may not see financial literacy as a core subject, believing that math, science, and language arts are more important for a student's future success. However, this mindset ignores the fact that no matter what career path a person chooses, they will need to understand how to manage their finances. Whether they become doctors, engineers, teachers, or artists, financial literacy is a universal requirement for success.

2.4 The Consequences for the Middle Class

The lack of financial literacy in schools disproportionately affects the middle class. Most middle-class families rely on their jobs for income and may not have the knowledge or resources to invest wisely. As a result, they remain stuck in a cycle of earning and spending without building substantial wealth. The education system, which prioritizes academic success and job security, does not equip them with the tools needed to break free from this cycle.

Many middle-class individuals follow a predictable path: they get a good education, find stable jobs, and spend their lives working to pay off mortgages, car loans, and credit card debt. They may save a portion of their income, but without a deep understanding of how to invest and grow their money, their wealth accumulation is slow, if not stagnant. Meanwhile, those who understand the power of compound interest, diversification, and risk management can significantly increase their wealth, even on modest incomes.

This financial illiteracy perpetuates a mindset of dependence on jobs and a paycheck-to-paycheck existence, making it difficult for middle-class families to achieve financial freedom.

2.5 The Role of Financial Education in Breaking the Cycle

To break this cycle, financial literacy must become a core part of the school curriculum. Teaching students how to manage money, budget, invest, and understand taxes should be as fundamental as teaching them to read and write. When students are taught financial principles early in life, they are more likely to make informed decisions about money, avoid debt traps, and take advantage of investment opportunities.

Some countries and states have begun introducing financial literacy programs, recognizing the importance of these skills for future generations. However, these efforts are still in the minority. A comprehensive financial education would include the following key areas:

- **Budgeting and Saving:** Understanding how to track income and expenses, create a budget, and save for both short-term and long-term goals.

- **Investing:** Learning the basics of investing, including stocks, bonds, mutual funds, and real estate, as well as understanding the risks and rewards of each.

- **Credit and Debt Management:** Knowing how to use credit wisely, avoid high-interest debt, and manage loans effectively.

- **Taxes and Retirement Planning:** Understanding how taxes work, how to file tax returns, and the importance of contributing to retirement accounts early in life to take advantage of compound interest.

2.6 Conclusion: A Call for Change

The omission of financial literacy from the school curriculum is a serious oversight that has lasting consequences for individuals and society as a whole. Without this knowledge, many people remain trapped in the middle-class cycle, working hard but never achieving true financial independence. It's time for education systems to recognize the importance of financial literacy and prioritize it in the same way they do other essential life skills.

By teaching students how to manage their money, invest wisely, and plan for the future, we can empower future generations to break free from the constraints of a paycheck-to-paycheck lifestyle and achieve financial freedom.

Understanding Income, Debt, and Basic Financial Concepts Schools Miss

In today's world, managing personal finances is a crucial skill, yet many people enter adulthood without a solid understanding of basic financial concepts. Schools often focus on traditional academic subjects but neglect practical financial education. As a result, individuals face a steep learning curve when it comes to managing their income, handling debt, and understanding fundamental financial concepts that impact their lives every day. This section explores the key areas that are often overlooked in school curricula but are essential for financial well-being.

1. Income: More Than Just a Paycheck

Most people understand income as the money earned through a job, whether it's a salary, hourly wage, or freelance work. However, the concept of income goes beyond simply collecting a paycheck. Schools often fail to teach students about the different types of income and how understanding these categories can help build wealth over time.

1.1 Earned Income

Earned income is the money individuals make through active work, whether as an employee, a business owner, or a freelancer. This is the most common form of income and is taxed heavily in most countries. Unfortunately, schools tend to focus on helping students prepare for jobs that generate earned income but rarely emphasize the downsides, such as the time-for-money trade-off and the limitations of relying solely on earned income for financial security.

1.2 Passive Income

Passive income refers to money earned with little or no effort after an initial investment of time, money, or resources. This could include rental income from properties, dividends from investments, or royalties from intellectual property like books or music. Schools rarely teach students how to generate passive income streams, yet it's one of the most effective ways to build wealth and achieve financial independence. Understanding the concept of passive income is essential for long-term financial stability, as it allows individuals to decouple their time from their earnings.

1.3 Portfolio Income

Portfolio income is the money generated from investments, such as stocks, bonds, and real estate. This form of income can grow significantly over time, especially when compounded. While schools often introduce students to saving money, they rarely dive into the mechanics of investing and growing a portfolio, leaving students with little knowledge of how to maximize their wealth through financial markets.

2. Debt: A Double-Edged Sword

Debt is another fundamental financial concept that schools overlook or, at best, only briefly touch upon. In reality, debt plays a significant role in many people's financial lives, and understanding how to manage it can mean the difference between financial success and ruin.

2.1 Good Debt vs. Bad Debt

Not all debt is created equal, yet schools often fail to make this distinction. **Good debt** refers to borrowing money for investments that will grow in value over time or increase your earning potential. For example, taking out a loan to buy a house or to finance an education can be considered good debt if it leads to long-term financial gains. On the other hand, **bad debt** is debt taken on for purchases that do not increase in value, such as credit card debt used for consumer goods. This type of debt often comes with high interest rates and can quickly spiral out of control.

Understanding the difference between good and bad debt is critical for making informed financial decisions. Schools should teach students how to assess whether a loan is beneficial in the long run and how to avoid falling into debt traps.

2.2 Interest Rates and Compounding Debt

One of the most important concepts that schools fail to emphasize is how interest rates work. Interest can either work for you or against you, depending on the context. For example, compound interest can be your best friend when you are investing or saving money, but it can become a nightmare when applied to debt. Many young adults enter the world of credit cards and loans without fully understanding how interest compounds, leading them to accumulate debt quickly.

If students were taught the power of compound interest early on—both its benefits when saving and its dangers when borrowing—they could avoid many of the financial pitfalls that plague so many adults.

2.3 Credit Scores and Their Impact

Another essential concept that schools often ignore is the **credit score**. Your credit score impacts your ability to borrow money, the interest rates you'll pay, and even your chances of securing housing or employment in some cases. Many individuals only learn about credit scores after they've already damaged theirs. Schools should teach students how credit scores are calculated, how to build a strong credit history, and how to repair a damaged score if necessary.

3. Financial Concepts Schools Miss

Beyond income and debt, there are several foundational financial concepts that schools should be teaching but typically do not.

3.1 Budgeting: A Core Life Skill

Budgeting is the cornerstone of financial management, yet it's rarely taught in schools. A budget helps individuals track their income and expenses, ensuring they don't spend more than they earn. Without a budget, many people end up living paycheck to paycheck, even if they have a decent income. Schools should teach students how to create and maintain a budget, helping them prioritize their spending, save for the future, and avoid unnecessary debt.

3.2 Emergency Funds: Preparing for the Unexpected

An **emergency fund** is a savings account set aside for unexpected expenses like medical emergencies, car repairs, or sudden job loss. Financial experts recommend saving three to six months' worth of living expenses in an emergency fund, yet most people don't have this safety net. Schools don't typically teach students the importance of having an emergency fund, leaving many young adults unprepared for life's financial curveballs.

3.3 Taxes: Understanding What You Owe and Why

Taxes are one of the few certainties in life, yet schools rarely prepare students for the realities of paying them. While most schools touch on the basics of income tax in social studies or economics classes, they rarely dive into the complexities of tax brackets, deductions, credits, and how to file a tax return. Students are often left to figure out taxes on their own when they enter the workforce, leading to confusion and mistakes. A basic understanding of how taxes work, how to minimize tax liabilities, and the importance of filing correctly would save many people unnecessary stress and financial trouble.

3.4 Inflation: The Silent Erosion of Wealth

Inflation is the gradual increase in prices over time, which reduces the purchasing power of money. While inflation might seem like a distant economic concept, it has a direct impact on personal finances. For example, money kept in a traditional savings account may lose value over time if the interest rate does not outpace inflation. Schools rarely address how inflation affects wealth and savings, leaving students with a limited understanding of how to protect their assets in the long run.

3.5 Retirement Planning: It's Never Too Early

Retirement may seem far off for students, but the earlier they start planning, the better off they'll be. Schools rarely teach students about retirement accounts like 401(k)s or IRAs, or the importance of contributing early and consistently to take advantage of compound interest. Without this knowledge, many people delay saving for retirement, only to find themselves playing catch-up later in life.

4. Conclusion: Filling the Gaps

The financial concepts of income, debt, budgeting, and saving are foundational to personal financial success, yet they are often left out of school curricula. Without this knowledge, many individuals make avoidable financial mistakes that can haunt them for years. By incorporating these essential financial lessons into education systems, we can equip future generations with the tools they need to manage their finances wisely, build wealth, and achieve long-term financial security.

It's time to rethink how we educate young people about money, ensuring they leave school not only with academic knowledge but with practical skills that will serve them throughout their lives.

CHAPTER 3

THE DANGERS OF RELYING SOLELY ON SALARIES

Why Relying on One Source of Income is Risky

In the traditional mindset, a stable, secure job with a fixed salary has long been seen as the ultimate goal, a symbol of success. For many, earning a regular income provides comfort and predictability. However, this mindset can also lead to one of the biggest financial traps—the danger of relying on a single source of income. Salaries, while seemingly stable, come with a set of inherent risks that few people acknowledge. Understanding these risks is critical to breaking free from the cycle that keeps individuals financially stagnant.

1. Job Security is an Illusion

No matter how secure your job may feel, job security is largely a myth. Economic downturns, industry disruptions, company restructuring, or even technological advancements can suddenly make a position redundant. Companies can and do lay off employees to protect their own interests. Many middle-class individuals have faced this harsh reality: despite years of service, they are often expendable when the company faces financial pressure.

Take the 2008 global financial crisis as an example. Millions of employees, who thought their jobs were secure, found themselves jobless overnight. While companies recover, individuals who rely solely on their salary often do not. Without multiple streams of income to fall back on, many people burn through their savings, accumulate debt, and find themselves trapped in a cycle of financial insecurity.

2. Limited Growth Potential

Salaries, by their very nature, limit how much one can earn. Most jobs offer a fixed monthly or yearly income with occasional increments or bonuses. This income growth is typically modest, not keeping pace with inflation or rising living costs. Furthermore, promotions or salary raises are often tied to the performance of the company, availability of higher positions, or subjective factors such as office politics.

Even highly qualified professionals, such as doctors, engineers, and teachers, often hit a ceiling in terms of salary growth. This limited earning potential makes it difficult to build wealth. Without exploring other income avenues, salary earners may find themselves living paycheck to paycheck, with little room for long-term financial growth.

3. The Impact of Inflation

Inflation is one of the silent threats to anyone relying solely on a salary. While salaries may increase annually by a small percentage, inflation tends to erode the real value of money. Over time, this diminishes the purchasing power of a fixed income, meaning you're essentially earning less in real terms each year.

For example, if your salary increases by 3% annually but inflation is running at 5%, you're effectively losing 2% of your purchasing power. This creates a financial squeeze that can make it difficult to maintain your lifestyle, let alone save for the future or invest. Those relying on just their salary are often unaware of how inflation quietly eats away at their wealth.

4. Unforeseen Expenses

Life is unpredictable, and unforeseen expenses such as medical emergencies, accidents, or family obligations can derail the best-laid financial plans. When you rely on one source of income, any large, unexpected expense can destabilize your financial situation. Salaries are designed to cover day-to-day living expenses, not large, unanticipated costs.

Individuals who only have their salary to depend on often resort to borrowing money, either through credit cards, loans, or family support. This, in turn, increases debt, leading to a vicious cycle of borrowing to cover costs and struggling to repay.

5. Lack of Financial Independence

When your entire financial well-being is tied to one employer or one source of income, you lose a degree of independence. Your livelihood depends entirely on the decisions of others, and that is inherently risky. Relying solely on a salary means that someone else is dictating how much you earn, and how often you get paid. If you lose that job, you lose your entire income.

True financial independence comes from diversifying your income streams. When you have multiple ways of generating income—whether through investments, side businesses, or real estate—you reduce your dependence on any one source. This diversification provides financial resilience and allows you to weather economic storms without compromising your lifestyle.

6. The Illusion of Stability

Salaries provide an illusion of stability. The comfort of receiving a paycheck every month can lull people into a false sense of security, making them complacent about their financial future. But stability should not be confused with financial growth. A salary can cover your basic needs, but it rarely provides the financial freedom to pursue passions, take risks, or invest in wealth-building opportunities.

Many people remain in jobs they dislike because they are afraid of losing their "stable" paycheck. However, this sense of stability is often a trap that keeps individuals from exploring entrepreneurial ventures, investments, or other opportunities that could generate higher income and long-term wealth.

7. The Opportunity Cost of Time

Relying solely on a salary means you're essentially trading time for money. You work a set number of hours each day or week in exchange for a fixed amount of income. However, time is a finite resource. There are only so many hours you can work in a day, which inherently limits how much you can earn.

What's more, this time could be better spent exploring other avenues of income, such as building a side business, investing in real estate, or learning about stock market investing. By focusing exclusively on salary-based work, individuals often miss out on opportunities to create passive income streams that don't require constant time input.

8. Tax Disadvantages

One often overlooked disadvantage of relying on a salary is the tax burden. Salaried income is taxed at a higher rate compared to other forms of income, such as capital gains from investments or business income. In many countries, tax brackets are structured in a way that disproportionately affects salaried individuals. The more you earn through your salary, the more taxes you pay, leaving you with less take-home income.

Conversely, individuals who earn income from businesses, investments, or property often benefit from tax advantages such as deductions, lower tax rates, and the ability to write off certain expenses. By diversifying your income streams, you can potentially reduce your tax burden and retain more of your hard-earned money.

9. The Importance of Diversifying Income

The antidote to the dangers of relying solely on a salary is diversification. Diversifying your income means creating multiple streams of income so that you're not dependent on just one source. This could include side businesses, real estate investments, dividend-paying stocks, or freelance work.

Diversification allows you to spread your financial risk. If one source of income dries up, you still have others to rely on. This not only provides financial security but also opens the door to greater wealth-building opportunities. Diversified income streams can help you build passive income, which allows your money to work for you rather than you always working for money.

How Salaries Limit Your Wealth Potential

Salaries, while providing a sense of financial security, inherently limit one's ability to accumulate wealth. Many people view a stable paycheck as the primary path to financial success, but this mindset can actually hold them back from achieving their full wealth potential. There are several ways in which relying on a salary restricts your financial growth, leaving you financially vulnerable in the long run.

1. Fixed Income Limits Earning Potential

The most obvious way that salaries limit wealth potential is through their fixed nature. Salaried employees are paid a predetermined amount each month, regardless of the amount of value they create for the company. This cap on earnings means that no matter how hard or efficiently one works, their income is restricted by the company's pay structure.

Even with raises, promotions, or bonuses, salary increases are usually incremental and often fail to keep pace with rising living costs or inflation. Moreover, most companies operate on an annual review basis, meaning your earnings are only reassessed once a year, limiting opportunities for significant income jumps.

2. Trading Time for Money

Salaries operate on the principle of trading time for money, which limits how much you can earn. Every employee has a finite number of hours in a day, and they are compensated based on the time they put in at work. This linear relationship between time and money creates a ceiling on how much one can earn, as there is only so much time available.

Additionally, because a salaried job requires consistent time commitment, there is little opportunity to explore other income-generating activities. When your income is tied directly to the hours you work, it leaves little room for passive income generation, where your money works for you, not the other way around.

3. Salaries Don't Account for Inflation

Inflation silently erodes the purchasing power of salaried income. Even if you receive an annual raise, it is often not enough to offset the rate of inflation. This results in a gradual decline in the real value of your salary over time, meaning that your earnings buy less each year. If inflation rises at 3% per year but your salary only increases by 2%, you're effectively losing purchasing power.

This is especially problematic for people who rely solely on their salary, as they may not realize how much inflation is eating into their wealth. Without investments that outpace inflation, salary earners find it harder to build wealth, as their savings lose value over time.

4. No Leverage for Financial Growth

One of the most powerful tools for building wealth is leverage—the ability to use other people's money, time, or resources to multiply your earning potential. Salaries, however, do not offer this opportunity. Employees are paid based on their individual efforts, without the ability to scale their income.

Entrepreneurs and investors, on the other hand, can leverage assets like business systems, real estate, or stock market investments to create exponential growth. By contrast, salaried workers are confined to a single stream of income that doesn't benefit from leverage, which stifles wealth accumulation.

5. High Tax Burden

Salaried income is subject to higher tax rates compared to other forms of income, such as dividends, capital gains, or business profits. In most countries, salaried workers are taxed at progressive rates, meaning the more you earn, the higher percentage of your income goes to taxes. This system disproportionately affects high-income salary earners, leaving them with less disposable income to save or invest.

In contrast, individuals who generate income through investments, property, or business ownership often benefit from more favorable tax treatment. Business owners can write off expenses, investors may pay lower taxes on long-term capital gains, and property owners can use depreciation to reduce their taxable income. Salaried workers, on the other hand, do not have access to these tax benefits, further limiting their wealth potential.

6. The Comfort Trap

One of the most subtle ways that salaries limit wealth potential is through the illusion of stability. A steady paycheck provides a sense of comfort, which can lead to complacency. When your basic needs are met by your salary, it becomes easy to settle into a routine and stop thinking about long-term financial growth. This comfort zone can prevent you from seeking out higher-risk, higher-reward opportunities that could significantly increase your wealth.

For many, the fear of losing their salary outweighs the potential benefits of exploring entrepreneurial ventures or investments. As a result, they remain in the same position for years, with little financial progress. The comfort trap keeps people locked into a cycle of earning just enough to get by, but not enough to break free from financial limitations.

7. Limited Control Over Income Growth

When you rely on a salary, your income growth is largely out of your hands. Raises, bonuses, and promotions depend on company policies, the state of the economy, and the decisions of your employer. This lack of control means that your financial success is often dictated by external factors, rather than your own efforts or decisions.

In contrast, individuals who run their own businesses or invest in various ventures have more control over how much they earn. They can scale their efforts, seek out new opportunities, and make strategic decisions to increase their income. This flexibility allows them to accelerate their wealth-building efforts, while salaried employees are often stuck waiting for the next promotion or raise.

Conclusion

While salaries provide a stable and predictable income, they also impose limitations on wealth-building. The fixed nature of salaried income, the lack of leverage, high tax burdens, and inflation all contribute to a financial ceiling that prevents many individuals from reaching their full wealth potential. To break free from these limitations, it's essential to explore other income streams, such as investments, entrepreneurship, or passive income, which offer greater control, flexibility, and opportunities for exponential financial growth.

CHAPTER 4

FINANCIAL LITERACY – THE ESSENTIAL KNOWLEDGE TO BUILD WEALTH

Financial literacy is the foundation of wealth-building. Without a solid understanding of core financial principles, individuals are left vulnerable to debt, poor decision-making, and stagnant wealth. Financial literacy empowers people to take control of their finances, plan for the future, and make informed decisions that can lead to financial independence. In this chapter, we will explore the four key areas of financial literacy: Budgeting, Saving, Debt Management, and Investing. Mastering these areas is essential for anyone seeking to escape the middle-class trap and build lasting wealth.

The Key Areas of Financial Literacy: Budgeting, Saving, Debt, and Investing

1. Budgeting: The Blueprint for Financial Control

Budgeting is the first and most fundamental aspect of financial literacy. It involves creating a plan that outlines your income, expenses, and savings. A well-structured budget helps you manage your money more effectively, ensuring that you live within your means while saving for the future.

Why Budgeting is Essential:

- **Awareness:** A budget gives you a clear picture of where your money is going. It prevents overspending and highlights unnecessary expenses.

- **Discipline:** Sticking to a budget requires discipline. It curbs impulse spending and encourages mindful financial decisions.

- **Goal Setting:** A budget helps you set financial goals, whether it's paying off debt, building an emergency fund, or saving for a major purchase.

Steps to Effective Budgeting:

- **Track Your Income and Expenses:** Start by recording all sources of income and every expense, no matter how small.

- **Categorize Your Spending:** Divide your expenses into essential (rent, utilities, groceries) and non-essential (entertainment, dining out).

- **Set Limits and Priorities:** Allocate a specific amount to each category and prioritize needs over wants.

- **Review and Adjust Regularly:** Life changes, and so should your budget. Regularly review it and make adjustments as needed.

An effective budget not only keeps your finances in check but also frees up money for saving and investing, accelerating your journey to wealth.

---

2. Saving: The Foundation of Financial Security

Saving is about setting aside a portion of your income for future use. While it may seem simple, saving is often the most overlooked component of personal finance. Without savings, you are vulnerable to financial shocks such as medical emergencies, job loss, or unexpected expenses. Establishing a habit of saving builds a safety net that can prevent you from falling into debt and gives you the capital to invest and grow your wealth.

Why Saving is Important:

- **Emergency Preparedness:** Life is unpredictable. An emergency fund helps cover unexpected expenses without derailing your financial stability.

- **Opportunity Fund:** Saving creates the foundation for future investments, enabling you to seize opportunities when they arise, such as starting a business or buying a home.

- **Peace of Mind:** Having money set aside reduces financial stress and allows you to focus on long-term goals instead of immediate crises.

Types of Savings:

- **Emergency Fund:** Ideally, you should aim for three to six months' worth of living expenses in an easily accessible account.

- **Short-Term Savings:** These are for planned expenses within the next few years, such as vacations or large purchases.

- **Long-Term Savings:** This includes retirement accounts or funds for major life goals like buying a home or funding education.

A strong savings habit is the cornerstone of financial independence. The more disciplined you are with saving, the more secure and prepared you will be for whatever life throws your way.

---

3. Debt Management: Taking Control of Your Financial Obligations

Debt can be a double-edged sword. On one hand, it can be a useful tool for financing large purchases like a home or education. On the other hand, mismanaged debt can lead to financial ruin. Understanding how to manage debt is a critical part of financial literacy.

The Dangers of Bad Debt:

- **High-Interest Rates:** Credit card debt and personal loans often come with high interest rates that can balloon your total debt if not managed properly.

- **Minimum Payments Trap:** Paying only the minimum amount on debt can keep you in a cycle of paying off interest without reducing the principal.

- **Damage to Credit Score:** Missed payments or carrying too much debt can lower your credit score, making it harder to borrow in the future.

Strategies for Effective Debt Management:

- **Avoid High-Interest Debt:** Minimize or eliminate credit card use and opt for lower-interest financing when necessary.

- **Pay More Than the Minimum:** To reduce the burden of debt, pay more than the minimum amount due each month.

- **Consolidate and Refinance:** Consider consolidating high-interest debts into one loan with a lower interest rate. Refinancing can also reduce monthly payments and total interest paid.

- **Prioritize High-Interest Debt:** Tackle high-interest debt first while maintaining minimum payments on lower-interest debt. This method, known as the "debt avalanche," reduces the overall interest you pay.

Debt can be a useful tool if managed wisely, but it is essential to differentiate between good debt (such as a mortgage or student loans) and bad debt (like high-interest consumer debt). Proper debt management ensures that you can borrow responsibly while minimizing the long-term financial burden.

---

4. Investing: The Key to Wealth Creation

Saving alone isn't enough to build significant wealth. To grow your money, you need to invest. Investing involves using your money to buy assets that have the potential to increase in value over time, such as stocks, bonds, real estate, or mutual funds. While investing comes with risks, it is one of the most effective ways to achieve financial independence.

Why Investing is Crucial:

- **Beating Inflation:** Money saved in a traditional savings account often doesn't keep up with inflation, eroding its purchasing power over time. Investing helps your money grow faster than inflation.

- **Compounding Returns:** The earlier you start investing, the more time your money has to grow through compound interest, where your returns generate even more returns.

- **Building Wealth:** Investing allows you to accumulate wealth over time, turning small amounts of money into significant assets.

Basic Principles of Investing:

- **Start Early:** The power of compounding means that time is one of the most important factors in successful investing. The earlier you start, the more your money will grow.

- **Diversify Your Portfolio:** Don't put all your eggs in one basket. Spread your investments across different asset classes to reduce risk.

- **Invest for the Long Term:** Successful investing is about patience. Avoid trying to time the market and instead focus on long-term growth.

- **Understand Risk Tolerance:** All investments come with risk. Assess your risk tolerance and invest accordingly. Higher-risk investments may offer greater returns, but they also come with the potential for losses.

Investing is the engine that drives wealth creation. By understanding and applying basic investment principles, you can grow your wealth exponentially over time.

Understanding How Money Works to Achieve Financial Freedom

Achieving financial freedom is the ultimate goal for many, but few truly understand the mechanics of how money works. Financial freedom means having enough income, investments, and savings to cover your living expenses without relying on a traditional job. It's about creating a life where money works for you, rather than you working for money. To reach this state, it's essential to understand key financial principles that govern wealth creation and management.

In this section, we will explore how money flows in and out of your life, the importance of cash flow management, the power of compounding, and the role of passive income in achieving financial freedom.

---

1. Understanding Cash Flow: The Lifeblood of Financial Freedom

Cash flow refers to the movement of money in and out of your personal finances. To achieve financial freedom, you need to have more money flowing in (income) than flowing out (expenses). The key is to manage and optimize cash flow so that a portion of your income is always directed toward wealth-building activities.

Positive vs. Negative Cash Flow:

- **Positive Cash Flow:** This occurs when your income exceeds your expenses. It provides the surplus necessary for saving, investing, and growing wealth.

- **Negative Cash Flow:** This happens when your expenses exceed your income. Negative cash flow forces you to dip into savings or take on debt, which hinders your ability to achieve financial independence.

Managing Cash Flow Effectively:

- **Track Your Spending:** Know where every dollar goes. Create a clear distinction between essential and discretionary spending.

- **Reduce Unnecessary Expenses:** Identify areas where you can cut back, such as subscriptions or dining out.

- **Increase Income Streams:** Focus on ways to increase your income, whether through career growth, side businesses, or investments.

By mastering cash flow, you take control of your financial destiny, ensuring that you always have money available to fuel your journey to financial freedom.

---

2. The Power of Compounding: Growing Your Money Exponentially

Albert Einstein once called compounding the "eighth wonder of the world." Compounding refers to the process by which your investments generate earnings, and those earnings, in turn, generate their own earnings. It allows your money to grow exponentially over time, making it one of the most powerful concepts in wealth-building.

How Compounding Works:

- **Interest on Interest:** When you invest money, you earn interest on your principal. As time passes, you also earn interest on the interest that has already accumulated.

- **Reinvestment:** Compounding works best when you reinvest your returns, allowing them to generate even more earnings over time.

Why Time is Your Best Ally:

- **Early Start:** The longer your money is invested, the more time it has to compound. Starting early, even with small amounts, can lead to significant growth over the long term.

- **Patience is Key:** Compounding requires patience. The initial growth may seem slow, but over time, the exponential effect becomes more visible and powerful.

For example, if you invest $10,000 at a 7% annual return, after 10 years, you'll have approximately $19,671. After 20 years, it grows to $38,697, and by 30 years, it reaches $76,122. The longer your money is invested, the more dramatic the growth.

---

3. Passive Income: The Pathway to Financial Freedom

One of the critical factors in achieving financial freedom is generating **passive income**—income that requires little to no effort to maintain once it's set up. Unlike active income, where you trade time for money (like a salary), passive income works in the background, allowing you to earn money even when you're not actively working.

Types of Passive Income:

- **Investments:** Dividends from stocks, interest from bonds, and capital gains from real estate are all forms of passive income.

- **Business Ownership:** Owning a business that doesn't require your daily involvement can generate passive income, especially if you delegate operations.

- **Royalties:** If you own intellectual property, such as books, music, or patents, you can earn royalties.

- **Rental Income:** Owning real estate and renting it out provides a steady stream of income without the need for daily involvement.

Why Passive Income is Crucial:

- **Financial Independence:** Passive income streams allow you to cover your expenses without relying on a job, creating financial freedom.

- **Flexibility:** Once established, passive income can free up your time to focus on other pursuits, whether that's personal development, family, or starting new ventures.

- **Wealth Accumulation:** The more passive income streams you have, the faster you can accumulate wealth. It reduces your dependence on active income and gives you financial security.

Building passive income takes time and effort in the initial stages, but once established, it can be the key to unlocking financial freedom.

4. Inflation and Purchasing Power: Protecting Your Wealth

Inflation is the gradual increase in prices over time, which reduces the purchasing power of money. Simply put, as inflation rises, each unit of currency buys fewer goods and services. Understanding inflation is crucial to financial freedom because it erodes savings that are not invested in growth-oriented assets.

How Inflation Impacts Wealth:

- **Erosion of Savings:** Money left in a regular savings account often earns interest below the rate of inflation, meaning your savings lose value in real terms.

- **Investment as a Hedge:** To beat inflation, your money must grow faster than inflation. This is why investing in stocks, real estate, or other assets is essential for maintaining and growing your wealth over time.

Protecting Against Inflation:

- **Invest in Assets:** Growth assets like stocks and real estate historically outpace inflation over the long term.

- **Diversify Globally:** Inflation can affect different economies at different rates. Diversifying your investments globally can provide a hedge against inflation in your home country.

By understanding and preparing for inflation, you can protect the value of your money and ensure that it continues to work for you in the future.

5. The Importance of Financial Education: Empowering Yourself to Succeed

To truly understand how money works and achieve financial freedom, ongoing financial education is key. The financial landscape is constantly changing, and staying informed about new investment opportunities, economic trends, and tax regulations can significantly impact your success.

Why Financial Education Matters:

- **Informed Decision-Making:** Financial literacy allows you to make informed choices, whether it's evaluating an investment, managing risk, or planning for retirement.

- **Avoiding Financial Pitfalls:** Many financial mistakes, such as taking on excessive debt or failing to invest, stem from a lack of understanding. Financial education helps you avoid these pitfalls.

- **Adapting to Change:** The world of finance is dynamic. Staying educated helps you adapt to changes in the economy, markets, and personal circumstances.

Invest in your financial education by reading books, attending seminars, following expert advice, and continually learning how money works. The more you know, the more empowered you are to take control of your financial future.

Conclusion: Achieving Financial Freedom by Mastering Money

Achieving financial freedom requires a deep understanding of how money works. By mastering cash flow management, harnessing the power of compounding, building passive income streams, protecting against inflation, and continuously educating yourself, you position yourself to live a life free from financial stress.

Financial freedom isn't a distant dream reserved for the wealthy. It is a goal that can be achieved by anyone with the right knowledge, discipline, and commitment. By learning to make money work for you, rather than the other way around, you take a powerful step toward creating the life you want—one of financial security, freedom, and abundance.

CHAPTER 5

DEVELOPING THE ENTREPRENEURIAL AND INVESTOR MINDSET

Shifting from an Employee to an Entrepreneur and Investor Mentality

The journey from financial struggle to financial freedom requires more than just knowledge and tools—it demands a fundamental shift in mindset. The way you perceive money, risk, and opportunity plays a pivotal role in determining whether you will remain trapped in the middle-class struggle or break free into a life of financial independence. At the heart of this transformation lies the shift from an employee mentality to an entrepreneurial and investor mentality.

1. The Employee Mentality: Seeking Stability and Security

From an early age, most of us are conditioned to believe that security comes from finding a stable job, earning a steady paycheck, and relying on a single source of income—our salary. The employee mentality is deeply ingrained in traditional education systems, which emphasize job security over risk-taking, stability over growth, and consumption over investing.

People with an employee mindset often focus on short-term rewards, such as monthly paychecks, job promotions, and benefits. They prioritize job titles and workplace recognition, often linking their self-worth to their roles within an organization. While these rewards offer comfort and security, they also come with limitations. Salaries are capped, and even the most dedicated employee can only earn so much within the constraints of their job.

Moreover, employees are often conditioned to trade their time for money, seeing time as their most valuable asset. This mindset can lead to burnout and frustration, as they must continually work to sustain their lifestyle. Time, however, is a finite resource, and relying solely on it for income limits one's potential for wealth creation.

2. The Entrepreneurial Mindset: Embracing Risk and Opportunity

The entrepreneurial mindset, on the other hand, sees the world differently. Entrepreneurs understand that true financial freedom comes from creating multiple sources of income, taking calculated risks, and viewing challenges as opportunities for growth.

Entrepreneurs don't just work for money; they make money work for them. They look for ways to scale their efforts, to generate income even when they are not actively working, and to leverage the power of systems, teams, and technology to multiply their efforts. Instead of being limited by the number of hours in a day, entrepreneurs aim to create businesses that generate wealth around the clock.

Risk is seen as an inherent part of this mindset. While employees tend to avoid risk in favor of security, entrepreneurs embrace it, understanding that the potential rewards far outweigh the risks if managed wisely. They constantly look for gaps in the market, unmet needs, and opportunities where they can innovate and create value.

Key traits of an entrepreneurial mindset include:

- **Problem-Solving:** Entrepreneurs see problems as opportunities to create solutions that add value.
- **Innovation:** They are constantly looking for new ways to improve existing systems or create entirely new products or services.
- **Adaptability:** Entrepreneurs are quick to pivot when circumstances change, always staying ahead of market trends.
- **Resilience:** Failure is seen as a learning experience rather than a reason to quit.

3. The Investor Mindset: Long-Term Wealth Building

While the entrepreneurial mindset focuses on creating value through businesses and innovation, the investor mindset is about making your money work for you over the long term. Investors understand that wealth is built through patience, strategic planning, and consistent investment.

Unlike employees, who often rely on a single source of income, investors diversify their income streams. They invest in assets that grow over time, such as stocks, real estate, businesses, and other income-generating vehicles. These investments not only provide passive income but also compound over time, allowing wealth to grow exponentially.

The key principles of the investor mindset include:

- **Delayed Gratification:** Investors prioritize long-term gains over short-term pleasures, understanding that real wealth takes time to build.

- **Risk Management:** Like entrepreneurs, investors understand the importance of risk but mitigate it through diversification and informed decision-making.

- **Compounding:** Investors take advantage of the power of compounding, where the returns on investments generate their own returns, leading to exponential growth over time.

- **Financial Education:** Investors are lifelong learners. They continuously educate themselves on market trends, financial instruments, and investment strategies.

4. Shifting from Employee to Entrepreneur and Investor

The shift from an employee mindset to an entrepreneurial and investor mindset requires a significant mental transformation. It involves breaking free from the traditional beliefs about work, money, and success that most of us have been taught. Here are the steps to begin this transformation:

Step 1: Change Your Relationship with Money

Employees often see money as a reward for their hard work, while entrepreneurs and investors view it as a tool to create more wealth. To shift your mindset, start thinking of money not as something to be spent but as something to be invested. Every dollar you earn is a seed that can grow if planted in the right place.

Step 2: Embrace Risk

To become an entrepreneur or investor, you must be willing to take calculated risks. This doesn't mean being reckless, but it does mean stepping out of your comfort zone. Whether it's starting a side business, investing in the stock market, or purchasing real estate, you must be willing to risk your time and resources to achieve greater rewards.

Step 3: Diversify Your Income

One of the greatest risks employees face is relying on a single source of income. If that income disappears, so does their financial stability. Entrepreneurs and investors, however, create multiple income streams. Start by identifying ways to generate income outside your job. This could include starting a side hustle, investing in dividend-paying stocks, or renting out a property.

Step 4: Invest in Your Financial Education

The most successful entrepreneurs and investors are those who never stop learning. Commit to lifelong learning about money, investing, and business. Read books, attend seminars, follow financial news, and seek out mentors who can help guide your journey.

Step 5: Think Long-Term

Both entrepreneurs and investors take a long-term view of success. They are not concerned with quick wins but are focused on building lasting wealth. Whether it's building a business or investing in the stock market, always prioritize long-term gains over short-term gratification.

5. The Freedom of Shifting Your Mindset

The ultimate reward of adopting an entrepreneurial and investor mindset is freedom. Freedom from the constraints of a job, freedom from the need to trade time for money, and freedom to pursue your passions and interests. Entrepreneurs and investors live life on their own terms, with the confidence that their wealth is working for them, even when they are not actively working.

This shift in mindset is not easy and requires consistent effort and learning. However, once you make the transition, the possibilities for growth and success are limitless.

How to Embrace Risk, Innovation, and Opportunity for Wealth Creation

The journey to financial success is never without risk. While many view risk as something to avoid, those who achieve significant wealth understand that risk is not an enemy—it is an essential ingredient for growth. By embracing risk, coupled with innovation and a keen sense of opportunity, individuals can create immense wealth. But how do you shift your mindset from fear to action? How do you see opportunity where others see uncertainty? This chapter will explore the methods for embracing risk, fostering innovation, and identifying opportunities for wealth creation.

1. Understanding Risk: The Foundation of Growth

Before embracing risk, it's important to understand its role in wealth creation. Risk is often perceived negatively because it carries the potential for loss. However, risk is also a pathway to reward. The key lies in **managing** and **calibrating** risk rather than avoiding it altogether.

There are different types of risk:

- **Financial Risk**: The potential loss of capital in investments or business ventures.
- **Career Risk**: Leaving a stable job or career path to pursue entrepreneurial ventures.
- **Market Risk**: Unpredictable shifts in market trends, customer behavior, or economic downturns.
- **Innovation Risk**: Creating new products, services, or systems that may or may not succeed in the market.

For most middle-class individuals, the fear of these risks often keeps them from taking action. However, successful entrepreneurs and investors see risk as an opportunity. They know that greater risk can lead to greater reward if handled strategically.

2. The Art of Calculated Risk-Taking

Taking risks doesn't mean jumping blindly into uncertain situations. Successful risk-takers practice **calculated risk-taking**. This involves analyzing the potential benefits versus the potential downsides and making informed decisions based on data, experience, and market research.

Here's how to become a calculated risk-taker:

- **Educate Yourself**: Before taking any major risks, gather as much information as possible. Whether it's investing in stocks, real estate, or launching a business, education is your first layer of risk mitigation. Understanding the industry, the market trends, and the key players gives you a significant advantage.

- **Start Small**: Begin by taking smaller, manageable risks. For instance, instead of quitting your job to start a business, begin with a side hustle. Invest a small amount in stocks before making larger investments. This builds your confidence and experience with risk.

- **Assess Potential Loss**: Always evaluate the worst-case scenario. Ask yourself, "What can I afford to lose?" If the answer is more than you are comfortable with, then scale down the risk or find ways to mitigate it.

- **Set Clear Goals**: Risk for the sake of risk leads nowhere. Be clear about your goals, whether it's a specific return on investment or market share for your business. This will help guide your risk-taking decisions.

- **Diversify**: Never put all your eggs in one basket. Successful investors and entrepreneurs spread their risk across different ventures, industries, or assets. This way, if one venture fails, the others still have the potential to succeed.

3. Innovation: The Key to Unlocking Opportunity

Wealth is rarely created by simply following what's already been done. It comes from innovation—finding new solutions to old problems, improving on existing products or services, or developing entirely new industries. To embrace innovation, you must first adopt a mindset that sees change as a positive force rather than a disruption.

How to Foster an Innovative Mindset:

- **Stay Curious**: The most innovative people are lifelong learners. They are always asking, "Why?" and "What if?" They challenge the status quo and question existing solutions. This curiosity drives them to explore new ideas and test unconventional methods.

- **Embrace Failure as a Learning Tool**: Innovation inherently comes with the risk of failure. However, failure is not the end—it's an important part of the process. Every failure provides valuable lessons that can lead to future success. Entrepreneurs like Elon Musk and Steve Jobs experienced multiple failures before achieving groundbreaking success.

- **Look for Gaps in the Market**: Some of the best opportunities for innovation lie in the gaps. Is there a product or service missing in your industry? Are there customer pain points that aren't being addressed? Successful innovators don't just create something new—they solve existing problems in a better way.

- **Collaborate**: Innovation often happens when diverse perspectives come together. Collaborating with people from different industries, backgrounds, or expertise can spark new ideas. Don't be afraid to partner with others or seek feedback from mentors and colleagues.

4. Identifying Opportunities: Where Others See Uncertainty

Opportunities for wealth creation are often hidden in plain sight. The ability to identify and seize these opportunities is what sets successful individuals apart. Whether it's a new market trend, a disruptive technology, or an underserved demographic, there are always opportunities waiting to be discovered.

Steps to Identify and Seize Opportunities:

- **Study Market Trends**: Pay attention to shifts in consumer behavior, technological advancements, and economic changes. Trends such as the rise of e-commerce, the shift toward remote work, or the increasing demand for sustainable products have created significant opportunities for those who identified them early.

- **Listen to Customers**: Customer feedback is a goldmine of opportunity. Often, consumers will express unmet needs or frustrations with current products or services. If you listen carefully, you can identify ways to innovate or create new solutions that cater to those needs.

- **Network Constantly**: Opportunities often arise through your connections. Attend industry conferences, seminars, or online forums where you can meet like-minded individuals and hear about emerging opportunities. Networking with other entrepreneurs, investors, or experts can open doors you never imagined.

- **Observe Disruptions**: Disruptions in markets often signal the birth of new opportunities. Whether it's a major technological breakthrough, new government regulations, or a global crisis, these events create shifts in industries that open doors for innovators and risk-takers.

- **Take Action**: The greatest opportunity in the world is useless if you don't act on it. Once you've identified an opportunity, take decisive action. This could mean investing in a new startup, launching a new product, or entering an emerging market. Remember, the window of opportunity is often small—those who act quickly reap the rewards.

5. Overcoming the Fear of Risk

For many, the greatest barrier to embracing risk is fear. Fear of failure, fear of losing money, or fear of the unknown can paralyze potential entrepreneurs and investors. However, fear can be managed and even used to your advantage.

Techniques for Overcoming Fear:

- **Change Your Perspective**: Instead of viewing risk as something to be feared, see it as a learning experience. Understand that failure is part of the process and that each setback is a step closer to success.

- **Break Risks into Small Steps**: You don't have to take one giant leap. Break down your risk into smaller, manageable actions. For example, instead of investing all your savings into one stock, spread it across several smaller investments.

- **Surround Yourself with Support**: Having a mentor or a supportive network can give you the confidence to take risks. Learning from others who have succeeded in risk-taking will inspire and guide you through your own journey.

- **Visualize Success**: Imagine what life will look like if the risk pays off. This mental exercise can help shift your focus from the fear of failure to the potential rewards of success.

Conclusion: The Intersection of Risk, Innovation, and Opportunity

Embracing risk, fostering innovation, and seizing opportunities are the pillars of wealth creation. Those who learn to balance these three elements unlock the potential to achieve financial freedom. The process requires courage, adaptability, and a willingness to step outside of your comfort zone. However, the rewards are well worth the effort. As you develop your ability to manage risk, think innovatively, and act on opportunities, you position yourself to create lasting wealth and success.

In the next chapter, we will explore practical strategies for diversifying income streams and building long-term wealth through multiple avenues, further solidifying your financial foundation.

CHAPTER 6

BUILDING MULTIPLE INCOME STREAMS

The Power of Passive Income: Real Estate, Stocks, and Businesses

In today's world, relying solely on one source of income, especially a salary, is no longer a safe bet. The financial landscape is unpredictable, jobs are not as secure as they once were, and relying on a paycheck limits your financial potential. The key to escaping the middle-class trap is to build multiple income streams—especially passive income. By creating streams of income that require little to no ongoing effort, you can achieve financial freedom and secure your future. This chapter explores three of the most powerful avenues for generating passive income: real estate, stocks, and businesses.

6.1 The Concept of Passive Income

Passive income is money earned with minimal effort or active involvement. Unlike your salary, which requires your time and presence, passive income continues to flow regardless of whether you're working actively or not. This kind of income frees up your time to focus on other ventures or simply enjoy life, while also protecting you from the risks of relying solely on one source of income.

The key to achieving financial independence lies in setting up these streams early and allowing them to compound over time. But before diving into how to build passive income through real estate, stocks, and businesses, it's important to understand why multiple streams of income are essential.

6.2 Why Building Multiple Income Streams is Critical

Having multiple income streams provides security and growth potential. Consider it a financial safety net: if one stream dries up, others can keep you afloat. For example, during an economic downturn, your salary might be at risk, but rental income or stock dividends could still provide support. This diversity protects your wealth and opens up opportunities for reinvestment and expansion.

Relying on only one source of income—like a traditional job—also limits your financial growth because your earning potential is capped. The hours in a day restrict how much you can work, but passive income streams are not bound by time. They can grow independently and exponentially.

Building multiple streams is the foundation for true financial freedom. Now let's explore how to create these streams in three powerful areas: real estate, stocks, and businesses.

6.3 Real Estate: Building Wealth through Property

Real estate has long been a favored avenue for passive income because it offers both consistent cash flow and long-term appreciation. There are several ways to generate income from real estate, each with varying degrees of effort and investment.

6.3.1 Rental Properties

One of the most straightforward ways to earn passive income through real estate is by owning rental properties. This could be residential homes, apartments, or commercial spaces. As a landlord, you receive rent payments from tenants. While being a property owner does require some initial capital and ongoing management (such as finding tenants and maintaining the property), it can become largely passive if outsourced to a property management company.

Rental income provides monthly cash flow, and over time, the property itself appreciates in value, contributing to long-term wealth. Additionally, there are tax benefits to owning real estate, such as deductions for mortgage interest and depreciation.

6.3.2 Real Estate Investment Trusts (REITs)

If you want to invest in real estate but don't have the capital or desire to manage properties, you can invest in Real Estate Investment Trusts (REITs). REITs allow you to buy shares in large real estate portfolios, and you earn dividends from the income generated by those properties. REITs are an excellent option for passive income because they require no direct involvement with property management and are accessible even with smaller amounts of capital.

6.3.3 Short-Term Rentals (Airbnb)

With the rise of platforms like Airbnb, short-term rentals have become a lucrative option. Renting out properties for short stays can generate more income than traditional leases, though it requires more hands-on management or the use of a property manager. This model works particularly well in high-demand tourist areas or business hubs. By investing in desirable locations, short-term rentals can be a high-return passive income strategy.

6.4 Stocks: Earning While You Sleep

Investing in stocks is another powerful way to build passive income. While the stock market can be volatile, disciplined, long-term investing allows your money to grow through dividends and capital appreciation.

6.4.1 Dividend-Paying Stocks

One of the easiest ways to earn passive income through the stock market is by investing in dividend-paying stocks. Companies with strong financials often return a portion of their profits to shareholders in the form of dividends. These dividends can be reinvested to buy more shares (further compounding your returns) or taken as cash to provide regular income.

Dividend investing is particularly appealing because it offers income regardless of whether the stock price is rising or falling. Many investors build portfolios entirely around high-quality dividend stocks, creating a stream of income that grows over time as companies increase their dividend payouts.

6.4.2 Index Funds and ETFs

Index funds and exchange-traded funds (ETFs) are another great way to build passive income through the stock market. These funds track a basket of stocks, usually from a specific index like the S&P 500, and allow you to benefit from the overall growth of the market without having to pick individual stocks.

Index funds and ETFs are popular because they are diversified, low-cost, and have a history of providing steady returns over the long term. Many of these funds also distribute dividends, offering both growth and income potential. They require minimal effort on your part, making them a great tool for passive income.

6.5 Businesses: The Ultimate Passive Income Machine

Starting or investing in businesses can be one of the most lucrative ways to build passive income. When structured correctly, businesses can operate with little to no involvement from you, generating income while you focus on other ventures or enjoy your freedom.

6.5.1 Building an Online Business

In today's digital age, building an online business is one of the most scalable ways to create passive income. From e-commerce stores to digital products, once the business is set up, it can generate income with minimal ongoing effort. For example, selling digital products like eBooks, online courses, or software can generate income continuously without the need for inventory or constant attention.

6.5.2 Franchises

Buying a franchise is another path to passive income through business ownership. Franchises come with a proven business model and established brand recognition, making them easier to manage. Many franchise owners hire managers to run the day-to-day operations, allowing them to focus on other ventures while the franchise generates income.

6.5.3 Silent Partnerships and Angel Investing

For those who don't want to run a business themselves, becoming a silent partner or angel investor is an attractive option. As a silent partner, you invest capital in a business and receive a share of the profits, but you're not involved in the daily operations. Angel investors provide funding to startups in exchange for equity, allowing them to earn returns if the business succeeds.

Both of these options allow you to earn passive income by leveraging someone else's efforts and expertise.

6.6 Combining Multiple Streams for Financial Freedom

Building wealth through passive income is not about choosing one path—it's about combining multiple streams. By investing in real estate, stocks, and businesses, you diversify your income sources and create a more stable financial foundation. Each stream complements the others, providing a buffer against economic uncertainty and amplifying your earning potential.

The goal is not just to replace your salary but to exceed it, giving you the freedom to pursue your passions, take risks, or retire early if you choose. The power of passive income lies in its ability to grow without your constant involvement, creating a self-sustaining system that works for you.

Diversifying Income to Maximize Wealth and Reduce Financial Risk

In the pursuit of financial freedom, the concept of diversification is key. Relying on a single income stream is not only risky, but it also limits your ability to build significant wealth. Just as you wouldn't invest all your money in one stock, you shouldn't depend entirely on one source of income. Diversifying income streams allows you to maximize wealth, protect against financial downturns, and reduce your reliance on any one source of earnings.

This chapter will dive into the importance of diversifying income, how it reduces financial risk, and how you can strategically diversify through various methods, including active, passive, and investment income sources.

---

1. The Importance of Diversifying Income

Diversifying income is about creating multiple ways to earn money so that you're not dependent on just one source. This can mean generating both active income (income that requires ongoing work, like a salary or freelance work) and passive income (income that continues to flow in with minimal effort, like rent from properties or dividends from stocks).

The core reasons for diversifying income are:

- **Financial Security:** If one income stream dries up, you have others to fall back on. This is crucial in times of job loss, economic downturns, or unexpected financial emergencies.

- **Wealth Accumulation:** By diversifying, you create opportunities for more growth. Different streams may provide varying levels of return, and having multiple sources increases your overall earning potential.

- **Flexibility and Freedom:** Multiple income streams allow you to reduce your dependence on a single employer or client, giving you the flexibility to explore new opportunities without the pressure of losing your primary income.

- **Protection Against Risk:** Different types of income respond to market fluctuations in different ways. Diversifying across industries, asset types, and revenue models reduces your exposure to any one market risk.

In essence, diversification spreads out your financial risk and increases your ability to achieve long-term financial stability and wealth.

---

2. How Diversification Reduces Financial Risk

The risk of relying on a single income stream is significant. Whether it's a salary, freelance income, or even a business you own, putting all your eggs in one basket is risky. Here's how diversifying your income protects you:

2.1 Economic Downturns and Job Losses

If your only income is from a job, you're vulnerable to job cuts, economic shifts, or industry-specific downturns. By having multiple income sources, such as investments in real estate or dividend-paying stocks, you are less likely to suffer the full brunt of a recession or unemployment.

2.2 Market Volatility

Investing in a single asset class or industry is risky because markets can be volatile. For instance, if you invest only in tech stocks and the tech sector crashes, your entire portfolio takes a hit. However, by diversifying across sectors (such as technology, healthcare, and real estate), you're better insulated from market fluctuations.

2.3 Personal Crises

In the case of personal crises, such as illness or family emergencies, active income sources (like a salary) can dry up if you're unable to work. Passive income streams, such as rental income or investments in dividend stocks, can continue to generate revenue even when you cannot work. This provides a safety net in difficult times.

---

3. Types of Income Streams to Diversify

The next step to diversifying your income is identifying the types of income streams you can create. A well-diversified income portfolio includes a mix of active, passive, and investment income.

3.1 Active Income

Active income requires direct participation, such as working a job or freelancing. While active income is crucial for most people to start with, it should not be the sole source of income over time. Examples of active income include:

- **Salary from Employment:** The most common form of active income, but also the most vulnerable to external factors.

- **Freelancing or Consulting:** A good way to supplement income with flexible work, though still reliant on active participation.

- **Side Gigs:** Using skills to create an additional income stream through part-time jobs or projects.

While active income is essential, the goal is to use it to fund other, more passive income-generating assets.

3.2 Passive Income

Passive income continues to flow with minimal effort after the initial setup. This type of income is ideal for financial independence because it grows without requiring your time. Some popular sources of passive income include:

- **Rental Properties:** Earn rental income from tenants while also benefiting from property appreciation over time.

- **Dividend Stocks:** Invest in companies that pay regular dividends to shareholders, providing consistent income without needing to sell the stock.

- **Peer-to-Peer Lending:** By lending money through peer-to-peer platforms, you can earn interest on the loans.

- **Royalties:** If you create intellectual property (e.g., books, music, software), you can earn royalties over time from its use or sale.

- **Digital Products:** Selling eBooks, online courses, or software is a scalable passive income stream that requires little maintenance after the initial product is created.

3.3 Investment Income

Investment income comes from assets like stocks, bonds, real estate, and other financial instruments. Investment income often forms the backbone of a diversified portfolio because it offers growth potential, income, and a way to compound wealth over time. Key examples include:

- **Stocks and Bonds:** Stocks offer growth potential and sometimes dividends, while bonds provide fixed-income returns.

- **Mutual Funds and ETFs:** Diversified portfolios of stocks, bonds, or other assets that offer growth and income with lower risk than individual securities.

- **Real Estate Investment Trusts (REITs):** Invest in real estate without owning physical property, earning income from commercial real estate portfolios.

- **Cryptocurrency:** A riskier, but potentially lucrative form of investment income, which should be considered only as part of a broader diversification strategy.

Each type of income comes with its own risks and rewards. By diversifying across active, passive, and investment income streams, you spread your risk and increase the likelihood of achieving your financial goals.

4. Strategies for Effective Income Diversification

Now that you understand the types of income streams, the next step is to develop a strategy for diversifying effectively. Here are some key strategies to maximize wealth and minimize risk:

4.1 Start with Your Strengths

Evaluate your current financial situation and skill set. If you have a secure job, start by adding passive income streams, such as investing in dividend stocks or real estate. If you're a freelancer, consider scaling by creating digital products or investing in income-generating assets.

4.2 Leverage Your Active Income

Use your active income to fund passive and investment income streams. Instead of spending all your earnings, allocate a portion to building assets that will generate future income. For example, save enough to purchase a rental property or build a stock portfolio that pays dividends.

4.3 Reinvest Income to Build Wealth

Reinvesting is a powerful way to accelerate your wealth-building efforts. Reinvest dividends, rental income, and business profits into additional investments. This strategy compounds your returns and creates a snowball effect, rapidly increasing your wealth.

4.4 Balance Risk with Return

Ensure your income streams are spread across a spectrum of risk levels. Higher-risk assets like stocks or businesses can provide substantial growth, but they should be balanced with safer investments like bonds, REITs, or rental properties to reduce volatility.

4.5 Continually Expand and Evolve

Building diversified income streams is not a one-time task. As your financial situation evolves, continue to seek new opportunities for income. Whether it's investing in new sectors, acquiring more properties, or starting a side business, continually expanding your income sources will help protect you from risk and maximize growth.

Conclusion

Diversifying your income is essential to maximizing wealth and minimizing financial risk. By creating multiple income streams through active, passive, and investment methods, you build a financial safety net that offers stability and long-term growth. This diversification allows you to weather financial storms, capitalize on opportunities, and, ultimately, achieve financial independence.

To reduce your reliance on any one income source, start by evaluating your strengths and gradually build new income streams over time. Whether it's investing in real estate, stocks, businesses, or digital products, a diversified approach will lead to sustainable wealth and greater financial freedom.

CHAPTER 7

LEVERAGING TECHNOLOGY FOR FINANCIAL GROWTH

How the Internet and Global Markets Provide Wealth-Building Opportunities

In the digital age, technology has fundamentally reshaped how we live, work, and, importantly, how we grow wealth. The internet and global markets have unlocked opportunities that were once accessible only to a privileged few. Today, with the right knowledge and strategy, anyone can take advantage of these tools to achieve financial growth.

1. The Democratization of Information and Finance

The internet has made financial knowledge more accessible than ever before. In the past, financial literacy was often restricted to those with access to specialized education or expensive financial advisors. Now, with a few clicks, you can access books, blogs, courses, and videos on personal finance, investing, and wealth-building strategies. Platforms like YouTube, blogs, and online courses provide a treasure trove of free or affordable content. This democratization of information has leveled the playing field, allowing people from all walks of life to learn and implement wealth-building techniques.

Moreover, financial markets that were once closed or limited to geographic regions are now global. With the rise of fintech and online trading platforms, you can invest in stock markets, commodities, and real estate from any part of the world.

2. The Power of Online Brokerage and Investment Platforms

Gone are the days when investing required a large capital outlay or a personal relationship with a stockbroker. Today, online brokerage platforms like Robinhood, E*TRADE, and Interactive Brokers allow individuals to start investing with minimal capital. These platforms provide access to a wide range of financial assets, including stocks, bonds, mutual funds, and even more sophisticated investment vehicles like options and futures.

Some platforms also offer commission-free trading, lowering the barriers for entry. This has created an unprecedented opportunity for everyday individuals to build wealth through stock market participation. Additionally, robo-advisors such as Betterment and Wealthfront use algorithms to provide personalized investment strategies, democratizing access to portfolio management.

3. Digital Currencies and Blockchain: New Frontiers of Wealth Creation

Cryptocurrencies and blockchain technology have emerged as powerful tools for financial growth. Bitcoin, Ethereum, and other digital currencies are providing new opportunities for wealth creation outside traditional banking systems. While volatile and speculative, those who have understood and embraced this new technology have reaped enormous financial rewards.

Beyond cryptocurrencies, blockchain technology itself is opening up opportunities for creating decentralized financial systems (DeFi), tokenized assets, and smart contracts, which have the potential to revolutionize real estate, intellectual property, and even the stock market. For the savvy investor, understanding blockchain and its applications could provide a significant financial advantage in the future.

4. Global E-commerce and Online Business: Turning Ideas into Income

The internet has also opened doors for individuals to create businesses with little upfront investment. E-commerce platforms like Amazon, Shopify, and Etsy enable entrepreneurs to sell products worldwide. Social media platforms such as Instagram, Facebook, and TikTok provide inexpensive ways to market products and services, reaching millions of potential customers without the need for traditional advertising.

In addition to selling physical products, online business models like dropshipping, affiliate marketing, and digital products (such as eBooks and courses) have become popular for those seeking to build multiple streams of income. This shift has allowed entrepreneurs to leverage technology to grow their businesses faster and more efficiently than traditional brick-and-mortar stores ever could.

5. Freelancing and the Gig Economy: Flexible Income Opportunities

With the rise of freelancing platforms like Upwork, Fiverr, and Freelancer, technology has provided a means for skilled individuals to offer services globally. Whether you're a writer, graphic designer, programmer, or marketer, these platforms allow you to connect with clients worldwide and build a location-independent career. This flexibility is particularly valuable for those looking to diversify their income streams while pursuing other financial goals, such as investing or starting a business.

Freelancing and the gig economy also allow individuals to monetize their skills and passions. For example, skilled photographers, videographers, or musicians can sell their work or offer their services directly to a global audience. The key to leveraging these opportunities is honing skills that are in demand and building a solid online presence.

6. Education and Continuous Learning: Leveraging Online Learning for Financial Growth

Technology also provides opportunities for continuous learning, a critical factor in staying competitive and growing financially. Online learning platforms like Coursera, Udemy, and Khan Academy offer courses on virtually any subject, including personal finance, investment strategies, and entrepreneurship. By leveraging these resources, individuals can continuously enhance their skills and knowledge, staying ahead of the curve in a rapidly changing world.

Moreover, some of the most valuable financial skills today, such as coding, data science, and digital marketing, can be learned entirely online. As industries evolve, the ability to quickly acquire and apply new skills is a crucial asset in growing wealth in the modern world.

7. Remote Work and the Global Workforce: Access to Higher-Income Opportunities

The rise of remote work has expanded income-earning opportunities beyond geographic borders. No longer are individuals limited to jobs in their local economy. With remote work, talented professionals can apply for jobs anywhere in the world, often earning higher wages than they would locally. Remote work has also provided opportunities for individuals to save money on commuting, meals, and other expenses, contributing to better financial management.

Additionally, for entrepreneurs and business owners, remote work has unlocked the possibility of hiring talent from all over the world. This allows businesses to scale quickly and affordably by tapping into a global pool of skilled workers.

8. Automation and AI: Optimizing Wealth Management

Advancements in artificial intelligence (AI) and automation are providing new tools to optimize wealth management. From automated budgeting apps like YNAB (You Need A Budget) and Mint to investment platforms using AI to forecast market trends, technology is helping individuals make smarter financial decisions. AI-powered tools can help identify patterns in spending, suggest saving strategies, and even automate investments based on risk tolerance and financial goals.

For businesses, automation has significantly reduced operational costs, allowing entrepreneurs to scale faster while focusing on strategic growth. Understanding how to incorporate automation tools can lead to more efficient wealth-building and financial management processes.

9. The Risks of Technology: Staying Informed and Vigilant

While technology offers numerous opportunities for financial growth, it also comes with risks. Cybersecurity threats, scams, and the volatility of digital currencies require individuals to stay informed and vigilant. It's important to understand the risks associated with new technologies and invest in securing your digital and financial assets.

In addition, while the accessibility of financial markets and platforms is empowering, it can also lead to impulsive or ill-informed decisions. It's essential to build a foundation of financial literacy before diving into more speculative investments or business ventures online.

Using Online Resources to Gain Knowledge and Create Wealth

The internet is a goldmine of information, tools, and platforms that can empower individuals to gain the knowledge necessary for wealth creation. From free educational content to structured courses and investment platforms, leveraging online resources is one of the most powerful ways to transform your financial situation. This chapter delves into how you can use these resources strategically to build your financial foundation, enhance your skills, and ultimately create wealth.

1. Access to Free Financial Education

One of the greatest benefits of the internet is the availability of free educational resources. Websites, blogs, YouTube channels, podcasts, and social media platforms offer a wealth of information on personal finance, investing, and entrepreneurship. These resources, created by experts, professionals, and experienced investors, are accessible to anyone with an internet connection.

Here are some ways you can use these free resources to expand your financial knowledge:

- **Blogs and Articles:** Personal finance blogs such as *The Simple Dollar*, *Mr. Money Mustache*, or *NerdWallet* provide insights on budgeting, saving, and investing. These websites offer detailed guides on practical financial strategies.

- **YouTube Channels:** Channels like *Graham Stephan*, *The Financial Diet*, or *Meet Kevin* offer free tutorials, step-by-step guides, and real-world experiences about personal finance and investing.

- **Podcasts:** Financial podcasts like *The Dave Ramsey Show* or *BiggerPockets Money Podcast* provide actionable advice and interviews with successful entrepreneurs and investors. You can listen to these during commutes or breaks, making learning flexible and accessible.

By consistently consuming this content, you can stay updated on financial trends, learn how to manage your money better, and explore various wealth-building strategies.

2. Structured Online Courses and Certifications

While free resources are an excellent starting point, structured online courses can provide a more in-depth understanding of complex financial topics. Platforms such as *Coursera, Udemy, LinkedIn Learning,* and *edX* offer courses on personal finance, stock market investing, entrepreneurship, and real estate. Many of these courses are designed by top universities and institutions, providing high-quality education at a fraction of the cost of traditional schooling.

Key benefits of online courses include:

- **Comprehensive Learning:** These courses are designed to take you from beginner to advanced levels in a systematic way. Whether you're learning about investment strategies or entrepreneurship, structured courses provide a curriculum that builds progressively.

- **Flexible Learning:** You can learn at your own pace, fitting education into your schedule. Many platforms offer lifetime access to course materials, enabling you to revisit lessons whenever necessary.

- **Affordable Certification:** Some platforms provide certificates upon course completion, which can boost your credibility if you're looking to start a career in finance or expand your qualifications.

For example, if you're interested in learning about stock market investing, you might enroll in *The Complete Stock Market Investing Course* on Udemy or take *Introduction to Finance* from a university on Coursera. These courses provide practical, actionable knowledge to build wealth in real-world scenarios.

3. Investment Platforms and Tools for Beginners

The internet has revolutionized how we invest by providing easy access to financial markets. Today, anyone with an internet connection can start investing with minimal capital using online investment platforms. This has leveled the playing field and allowed everyday people to grow their wealth without needing large sums of money or access to exclusive brokers.

Here are some of the top investment platforms available to beginners:

- **Stock Trading Platforms:** Apps like *Robinhood*, *ETRADE**, and *Fidelity* allow users to trade stocks, ETFs, and other securities directly from their phones. Many offer commission-free trading, making it affordable for beginners to start investing without being burdened by high fees.

- **Robo-Advisors:** Platforms such as *Betterment* and *Wealthfront* use algorithms to create and manage a diversified investment portfolio tailored to your risk tolerance and financial goals. Robo-advisors automate the investment process, making it easy for beginners who may not have in-depth knowledge of the stock market.

- **Real Estate Crowdfunding:** Platforms like *Fundrise* and *Roofstock* allow individuals to invest in real estate properties with relatively small amounts of capital. By pooling funds from multiple investors, these platforms make real estate accessible to those who may not have the money to buy properties on their own.

These platforms provide educational tools to help you understand your investments, and many offer demo accounts for beginners to practice trading without risking real money.

4. Online Communities and Forums

Learning from a community of like-minded individuals can accelerate your financial growth. Online forums and social media groups provide platforms where people share their experiences, ask questions, and exchange knowledge about personal finance, investing, and entrepreneurship.

Popular online communities include:

- **Reddit's r/personalfinance** and **r/investing:** These subreddits are filled with discussions, advice, and resources on managing money and building wealth. You can learn from others' mistakes, successes, and strategies while asking questions that pertain to your specific situation.

- **Facebook Groups:** Groups such as *Financial Independence Retire Early (FIRE)* or *Personal Finance and Investing* are excellent for engaging with people who share similar financial goals. These groups often host live Q&A sessions, webinars, and share up-to-date news on financial opportunities.

- **BiggerPockets Forums:** For those interested in real estate investing, BiggerPockets provides a wealth of knowledge through its community-driven forums. From beginner to expert, investors share their real estate strategies and experiences.

Being active in such communities not only keeps you informed but also connects you to mentors and peers who can guide you on your financial journey.

5. Leveraging Social Media for Business and Income

Social media platforms like Instagram, Facebook, LinkedIn, and TikTok aren't just for entertainment—they can also be powerful tools for creating wealth. Entrepreneurs, freelancers, and business owners can use these platforms to market their products, build personal brands, and attract clients.

Here's how you can use social media to create wealth:

- **Building a Personal Brand:** Platforms like LinkedIn allow you to establish yourself as an expert in your field, attracting clients and business opportunities. Posting insightful content, networking with professionals, and engaging with others can enhance your credibility and marketability.

- **E-commerce Sales:** Social media can drive traffic to your online store. Instagram and Facebook offer shops and marketplace features that allow you to sell products directly to your audience. By mastering digital marketing strategies, you can grow your e-commerce business and generate substantial income.

- **Monetizing Content:** If you have a following on platforms like YouTube or TikTok, you can monetize your content through ad revenue, sponsorships, and affiliate marketing. Content creators who educate or entertain their audience can generate significant income while building a loyal fan base.

Using social media strategically as part of your wealth-building plan can open up new streams of income while expanding your network and visibility.

6. Developing In-Demand Skills through Online Learning

The rise of online learning platforms has made it easier than ever to acquire high-demand skills that can significantly increase your income potential. Whether you're looking to enhance your career, start a side hustle, or launch a new business, the skills you can learn online are often the key to unlocking financial success.

Some of the most valuable skills you can learn online include:

- **Coding and Software Development:** With the tech industry booming, learning to code is one of the most lucrative skills you can acquire. Platforms like *Codecademy*, *Udacity*, and *freeCodeCamp* offer coding courses that can lead to high-paying jobs or freelance opportunities.

- **Digital Marketing:** Understanding how to market products and services online is crucial in today's business landscape. Courses on *Udemy* and *Google Digital Garage* provide training on SEO, social media marketing, email marketing, and more.

- **Data Analysis and Machine Learning:** As data becomes increasingly important across industries, learning how to analyze and interpret data can set you up for success. Websites like *DataCamp* and *Coursera* offer courses on data science, machine learning, and artificial intelligence.

Investing in these skills through online learning platforms can increase your earning potential and open doors to new wealth-building opportunities.

Conclusion

The internet has revolutionized the way we learn, invest, and build wealth. By leveraging online resources, individuals can access a world of knowledge, tools, and opportunities that were once available only to the elite. From free educational content and structured online courses to investment platforms and social media marketing, the internet offers countless ways to grow your wealth.

However, success requires a commitment to continuous learning, the discipline to apply what you've learned, and the foresight to take calculated risks. With the right mindset and the strategic use of online resources, anyone can start on the path to financial independence. The key is to take action—start learning, start investing, and start building the wealth you deserve.

CHAPTER 8

CASE STUDIES OF FINANCIAL TRANSFORMATION

How Individuals Broke Free from the Education Trap and Built Wealth

In this chapter, we'll explore the journeys of individuals who escaped the limitations of traditional education and built significant wealth. These real-life examples demonstrate that breaking free from the education trap is possible by adopting an entrepreneurial mindset, pursuing financial literacy, and leveraging opportunities beyond conventional career paths.

1. The Engineer Turned Investor: Aman's Story

Aman had a typical middle-class upbringing. He excelled in school, secured a degree in engineering, and found a stable job at a multinational corporation. Aman followed the standard script: study hard, get a degree, and find job security. For years, he enjoyed a steady paycheck but eventually felt trapped by the limitations of a single income source and the pressure to maintain his lifestyle through salary alone.

At the age of 35, Aman began reading books on personal finance, including "Rich Dad, Poor Dad" by Robert Kiyosaki. Inspired, he shifted his focus from being a salaried employee to becoming an investor. He started investing in stocks and mutual funds, gradually building his financial knowledge through self-study and by attending financial seminars.

Over time, Aman diversified his investments, incorporating real estate and dividend-paying stocks into his portfolio. His goal was to create multiple streams of income so that he wouldn't rely solely on his salary. Within ten years, Aman had built substantial passive income that allowed him to retire early and focus on new entrepreneurial ventures. His journey showcases the power of financial literacy and investing as a means of escaping the education trap.

2. The School Teacher Who Built an E-commerce Business: Priya's Story

Priya was a high school teacher who loved her job but realized early on that her salary would never allow her to achieve financial freedom. While she enjoyed the stability and fulfillment of teaching, she also desired more control over her financial future.

One day, Priya stumbled across a YouTube video about selling products online through e-commerce. She was intrigued by the potential of building a business outside of her 9-to-5 job. With no prior business experience, Priya began learning about e-commerce, marketing, and online sales. She started small, selling handmade crafts on platforms like Etsy and Amazon.

Over time, her side hustle began to grow, and she reinvested her profits into expanding her product line. Priya eventually launched her own website, focusing on niche products she was passionate about. Within five years, she was making more from her online business than from her teaching job. She eventually transitioned out of teaching to focus on her business full-time.

Priya's success highlights the importance of pursuing entrepreneurial opportunities alongside traditional employment. By breaking free from the education trap, Priya built a thriving business that provided her with financial independence.

3. The College Dropout Who Mastered Digital Marketing: Rahul's Story

Rahul struggled academically in college and ultimately dropped out, much to his parents' disappointment. Labeled a failure by his peers, Rahul's prospects seemed bleak. However, instead of wallowing in regret, he decided to learn a practical skill that was in high demand: digital marketing.

Rahul took online courses on social media marketing, SEO, and paid advertising, gaining expertise in an industry that traditional education barely touched on. After mastering these skills, Rahul started freelancing for small businesses, helping them grow their online presence.

Within two years, he built a successful digital marketing agency with clients from around the world. His business grew rapidly, and he expanded his services to include website design and branding. Today, Rahul is financially independent and runs a thriving company that generates a six-figure income. His story exemplifies how mastering skills not typically taught in school can lead to financial transformation.

4. The Couple Who Built Wealth through Real Estate: Anjali and Raj's Story

Anjali and Raj, both government employees, had steady jobs with modest salaries. Despite their financial stability, they realized they were stuck in the middle-class trap, relying solely on their incomes and pensions for retirement.

They began attending real estate investment seminars to learn about building wealth through property. Although initially hesitant, they made their first investment in a small rental property. Over the next few years, they acquired more properties, reinvesting rental income into further acquisitions. By the time they were in their mid-40s, they had built a portfolio of rental properties that generated enough passive income to match their salaries.

Anjali and Raj eventually left their government jobs and became full-time real estate investors. They demonstrated that even individuals with no prior business background can break free from the education trap by leveraging real estate to create wealth.

5. The Corporate Professional Turned YouTube Entrepreneur: Suman's Story

Suman followed a traditional career path, working as a marketing executive for a large corporation. Despite being successful, she felt unfulfilled and was frustrated by the limited upward mobility in her job. She started a YouTube channel as a hobby, creating content about personal finance and career development.

Her channel quickly gained popularity, and she monetized it through ads, sponsorships, and affiliate marketing. Suman continued working at her corporate job while growing her YouTube presence, but within two years, her side hustle was generating more income than her full-time job.

She eventually quit her job to focus on her YouTube channel full-time, using her platform to help others improve their financial literacy. Suman's story highlights how leveraging digital platforms and content creation can lead to financial freedom, even for those starting from a corporate background.

These case studies illustrate that breaking free from the traditional education trap is not only possible but also achievable through diverse paths. The key commonalities among these success stories are the pursuit of financial literacy, entrepreneurial thinking, and the willingness to take risks outside the confines of a conventional job. Each individual transformed their financial reality by seeking knowledge beyond the classroom and applying it to real-world opportunities.

Here are famousl stories of individuals who became rich by embracing financial literacy, entrepreneurship, and investment, illustrating how they used their knowledge and skills to break free from traditional paths to success:

1. Warren Buffett: The Investor Who Mastered Compounding

Warren Buffett is one of the most successful investors of all time, often referred to as the "Oracle of Omaha." His wealth-building story is rooted in financial literacy and the principles of compounding. Buffett began investing at the age of 11, buying three shares of stock in Cities Service for $38 each. Even at this young age, he understood the importance of starting early.

Buffett's strategy was simple: invest in undervalued companies, hold for the long term, and reinvest dividends. He continued to build his wealth over the decades through Berkshire Hathaway, a holding company he used to acquire businesses like Coca-Cola, American Express, and Geico. By applying the principles of value investing and staying patient, Buffett turned small initial investments into billions of dollars.

Key Lessons:

- The power of compound interest.
- Investing in businesses with strong fundamentals.
- Long-term patience in the stock market.

2. Sara Blakely: The Entrepreneur Who Built a Billion-Dollar Business

Sara Blakely, the founder of Spanx, became a self-made billionaire by solving a simple problem many women face: uncomfortable and unflattering undergarments. Before her entrepreneurial success, Blakely worked as a door-to-door fax machine salesperson. Despite facing numerous rejections, she saved $5,000 and used it to develop a prototype for her innovative undergarments.

Blakely embraced financial literacy and entrepreneurial thinking by focusing on solving a real-world problem and understanding her market. She was persistent and resourceful, initially handling all aspects of the business herself, from product development to marketing. Spanx eventually gained attention after Oprah Winfrey featured the product on her show, catapulting Blakely's business to massive success.

Key Lessons:

- Solving a real problem can lead to wealth.
- Resourcefulness and persistence are critical in entrepreneurship.
- You don't need to start with a large investment to build a billion-dollar business.

3. Elon Musk: The Innovator Who Invested in Multiple Industries

Elon Musk, the founder of Tesla, SpaceX, and other groundbreaking companies, became one of the wealthiest people in the world through entrepreneurship and investment. Musk's journey began when he co-founded Zip2, an online city guide software company that he sold for nearly $300 million. He then co-founded X.com, an online payment company, which eventually became PayPal and was acquired by eBay for $1.5 billion.

Instead of resting on his initial success, Musk reinvested his wealth into ambitious ventures like SpaceX and Tesla Motors, companies that aimed to revolutionize space exploration and the electric vehicle market. His relentless pursuit of innovation and willingness to take risks made him a billionaire. Musk used his financial knowledge to bet big on industries that had enormous potential for future growth.

Key Lessons:

- Diversifying investments across industries can lead to significant wealth.
- Taking calculated risks is essential for large-scale entrepreneurial success.
- Innovation and long-term vision are keys to building a fortune.

4. Robert Kiyosaki: The Advocate of Financial Literacy

Robert Kiyosaki, author of the best-selling book *Rich Dad, Poor Dad*, built his wealth by educating others about financial literacy. In the book, he compares the advice of his "poor dad" (his biological father, who valued traditional education) with that of his "rich dad" (his friend's father, who taught him about investing and entrepreneurship). Kiyosaki's central message is that traditional education does not teach the financial skills necessary to achieve wealth.

Kiyosaki became financially independent through investments in real estate, which provided him with passive income streams. He used the cash flow from his properties to fund other ventures, emphasizing the importance of owning assets that generate income. Today, Kiyosaki is not only wealthy from his real estate investments but also from his books, seminars, and financial education business.

Key Lessons:

- Financial literacy is essential for wealth creation.

- Investing in income-generating assets, like real estate, provides financial security.

- Education about money management is critical for long-term wealth.

5. Oprah Winfrey: The Media Mogul Who Built a Billion-Dollar Empire

Oprah Winfrey's rise from poverty to becoming one of the richest women in the world is a testament to the power of entrepreneurship and self-investment. Winfrey's career began in radio and television, but she transformed herself into a media mogul by launching her own production company, Harpo Productions. This move allowed her to control the rights to her shows and content, generating significant wealth.

Oprah embraced financial literacy by understanding the importance of ownership in business. She reinvested her earnings into her production company, various media projects, and philanthropic endeavors. In addition to her work in media, Winfrey has diversified her investments into sectors like education and health, further expanding her wealth.

Key Lessons:

- Ownership and control of intellectual property are key to financial success.

- Diversifying investments across industries helps secure long-term wealth.

- Building a brand around personal values and vision can lead to entrepreneurial success.

6. Tony Robbins: The Financial Educator and Entrepreneur

Tony Robbins, a world-renowned life coach and motivational speaker, built his fortune by mastering both entrepreneurship and financial literacy. Robbins started his career in personal development, but his wealth exploded when he expanded into other areas, including finance. Through his seminars and best-selling books, Robbins has taught millions of people the principles of financial independence.

Robbins has partnered with financial experts like Ray Dalio to educate the public about investing, saving, and achieving financial freedom. His focus on empowering people through financial education has not only helped his audience but also built his own wealth through various business ventures, including financial coaching programs and investments in multiple industries.

Key Lessons:

- Financial literacy is crucial for achieving financial independence.
- Diversifying revenue streams across different industries is essential for long-term wealth.
- Education and empowerment can be powerful tools for wealth creation.

These real-life stories demonstrate the transformative power of financial literacy, entrepreneurship, and investment. Each individual started from different backgrounds, but by educating themselves about money, embracing entrepreneurship, and making smart investments, they broke free from traditional paths and achieved extraordinary wealth. The common threads in their journeys are financial education, strategic risk-taking, and a focus on building long-term, sustainable wealth.

CHAPTER 9

FROM CORPORATE EMPLOYEE TO FINANCIAL FREEDOM

Real-Life Examples of People Who Shifted from a Job-Oriented Life to Building Passive Income Streams

Many corporate employees dream of financial freedom but feel trapped by the constraints of their jobs. The daily grind, the limited vacation time, and the reliance on a single source of income can create a feeling of entrapment. However, some individuals have successfully broken free from this cycle, transitioning from job-dependent workers to financially independent individuals by building passive income streams. This chapter will highlight several real-life examples of people who made this shift, illustrating how it is possible to escape the corporate rat race and achieve financial independence.

---

1. John Smith: Turning Real Estate Investments into Financial Freedom

John Smith spent 15 years working as an accountant in a large corporation. Like many middle-class workers, he found himself climbing the corporate ladder, but despite promotions and salary increases, he realized that he was still living paycheck to paycheck. His salary, while comfortable, was consumed by expenses, and the dream of early retirement seemed impossible.

John's financial transformation began when he read a book on real estate investing. He started small, purchasing a single rental property with the help of a mortgage. Over the years, John reinvested the rental income into additional properties, steadily growing his portfolio.

His key strategy was focusing on properties that could generate strong cash flow while requiring minimal management. He automated much of the property management process by hiring a management company, turning his real estate business into a relatively passive income stream. Within ten years, John had built enough passive income to replace his corporate salary. Today, he enjoys financial freedom, traveling the world while continuing to grow his real estate portfolio.

Key Takeaways:

- Start small but stay consistent.
- Reinvest income to grow your portfolio.
- Automate where possible to make your income streams truly passive.

2. Sara Patel: Building a Digital Business for Passive Income

Sara Patel spent over a decade working in marketing at a Fortune 500 company. Despite her success in her career, Sara found herself burnt out and dreaming of financial independence. She wanted to escape the long hours and stress of corporate life, but she wasn't sure how.

Her journey toward financial freedom started when she began building an online business on the side. Sara launched a blog that focused on digital marketing strategies for small businesses. She monetized her blog through affiliate marketing, selling digital products such as eBooks and online courses, and running paid advertisements.

Sara invested her evenings and weekends into her business for the first two years. As her blog traffic grew, so did her revenue streams. Soon, the income from her blog surpassed her corporate salary. She made the leap and quit her job to focus full-time on her online business.

Today, Sara's digital marketing blog generates passive income, allowing her to work on passion projects, travel, and live life on her own terms. Her business continues to grow as she expands into new online ventures.

Key Takeaways:

- Side hustles can eventually replace your main income.
- Online businesses offer scalable income with minimal overhead.
- Diversify revenue streams within your business (affiliate marketing, digital products, etc.).

---

3. Michael Johnson: Investing in Stocks and Building Dividend Income

Michael Johnson was a software engineer who loved his job but wanted more financial security. He realized early on that relying solely on his salary was risky, especially as he started thinking about retirement and the unpredictable nature of the job market.

Michael decided to educate himself on stock market investing. Instead of trying to time the market or make risky investments, he focused on building a diversified portfolio of dividend-paying stocks. He started small, investing a portion of his income each month into these stocks.

Over time, the dividends started to compound. By reinvesting his earnings, Michael's portfolio grew, and so did his passive income. After years of disciplined investing, Michael found that the income from his dividend portfolio was enough to cover his living expenses. While he still enjoys working, he now has the financial flexibility to take time off, explore other interests, and pursue new projects without the stress of financial instability.

Key Takeaways:

- Dividend stocks can provide a reliable source of passive income.

- Reinvesting dividends accelerates the growth of your portfolio.
- Consistent, long-term investing is key to financial freedom.

---

4. Linda and Robert Carter: Building a Family Business and Creating Multiple Income Streams

Linda and Robert Carter were both high-earning professionals in the tech industry, but the long hours and demanding nature of their jobs left little time for their family. They wanted more flexibility in their lives and a path to financial independence that wouldn't leave them tied to their corporate jobs.

Together, they decided to start a family business: a health and wellness company that sold organic skincare products. They began by selling their products online, utilizing e-commerce platforms like Amazon and Shopify. As the business grew, they expanded into wholesale and eventually opened their own storefront.

Linda and Robert outsourced many of the operational tasks to employees, allowing them to focus on high-level strategy and business growth. Their business not only provided them with significant passive income, but it also gave them the flexibility to spend more time with their children and pursue personal interests.

Today, the Carters have multiple income streams from their e-commerce business, investments in real estate, and a portfolio of stocks. They've achieved financial freedom and have the flexibility to choose how they spend their time.

Key Takeaways:

- Starting a family business can provide both financial freedom and flexibility.

- Diversify your income streams to reduce risk and increase financial stability.

- Outsourcing and automating can turn a business into a passive income stream.

---

5. David Lee: Using the Gig Economy to Build Income Streams

David Lee worked as an engineer for 20 years before realizing that his job wasn't fulfilling him. He wanted the freedom to work on his own terms and pursue creative interests. David took a leap of faith and left his corporate job, but instead of relying on a single new venture, he began building multiple streams of income in the gig economy.

David started freelance consulting in his area of expertise, but he also took advantage of platforms like Airbnb, renting out a portion of his home for extra income. He diversified further by investing in peer-to-peer lending and creating online courses that taught engineering principles. Each of these ventures created small, but steady income streams, which collectively allowed him to live comfortably without the need for a traditional job.

Key Takeaways:

- The gig economy offers opportunities to create multiple small income streams.

- Don't rely on one source—diversification is key.

- Be open to trying different ventures to find what works best for your lifestyle.

Conclusion

These real-life examples demonstrate that financial freedom is possible even for those who start out in a traditional corporate job. Whether through real estate, online businesses, stock market investing, or creating multiple streams of income through the gig economy, the path to financial independence requires a shift in mindset from relying solely on a salary to building passive income.

The key to success in these examples lies in taking consistent action, diversifying income streams, and using passive income sources to gain the freedom to live life on your own terms.

CHAPTER 10

THE SELF-EDUCATION PATH TO WEALTH

How Self-Education in Financial Literacy and Investing Created Wealth for Non-Traditional Learners

1. Introduction to Self-Education and Its Importance

In today's rapidly changing financial landscape, the role of self-education has become more crucial than ever. While traditional education lays the foundation for basic knowledge and skills, it often falls short in preparing individuals for the complex financial decisions they'll face throughout their lives. Self-education, on the other hand, is a powerful tool that empowers people to bridge the gap between what is taught in schools and what is necessary to thrive in the real world—especially when it comes to building wealth.

Definition of Self-Education

Self-education refers to the process of learning beyond formal education systems. It is a proactive approach where individuals take charge of their learning, seeking out resources, knowledge, and experiences that formal education may overlook. In the realm of financial literacy and investing, self-education can mean reading books, attending seminars, following financial experts, and utilizing online resources to gain an in-depth understanding of personal finance, investing, and wealth-building strategies.

Why Self-Education Matters in Financial Success

The traditional education system often emphasizes earning a salary through a job, but rarely does it teach students how to manage that salary, invest it, or build multiple streams of income. This is where self-education comes into play. Many wealthy individuals owe their success not to formal schooling, but to the knowledge and skills they acquired through self-education. Financial success is less about formal qualifications and more about understanding how to use money to create more wealth. Self-education provides the flexibility to explore these topics in-depth, at your own pace, and tailored to your unique financial goals.

The Advantages of Self-Education in a Rapidly Evolving Financial Landscape

The financial world is changing faster than ever before. The rise of digital currencies, global markets, decentralized finance (DeFi), and online trading platforms means that opportunities for building wealth are more diverse but also more complex. Traditional education systems struggle to keep up with these rapid advancements, leaving many individuals ill-prepared for new financial realities. Self-education, however, allows people to stay informed, adapt quickly, and leverage the latest financial tools and trends to their advantage.

By taking control of their learning, non-traditional learners can tap into wealth-building strategies that are often ignored or misunderstood by those who rely solely on traditional education. In this chapter, we'll explore how self-education in financial literacy and investing has helped countless individuals break free from the constraints of the education system and achieve financial independence.

2. The Gaps Left by Traditional Education

One of the primary reasons many individuals struggle financially is the significant gap between what is taught in traditional education systems and what is needed to thrive in the real world. Despite spending years in school, most people graduate without the practical financial knowledge necessary to manage money effectively, build wealth, or navigate the complexities of modern financial systems.

Lack of Practical Financial Knowledge in Formal Schooling

In schools, subjects like mathematics, science, and history are given priority, but essential life skills—particularly financial literacy—are often overlooked. The few topics that do touch on finance, such as basic economics or business studies, tend to focus on theory rather than practical applications. As a result, young adults enter the workforce knowing how to solve algebraic equations or write essays, but they have little understanding of how to budget, invest, or manage debt. The absence of formal education on topics like saving for retirement, understanding credit, or building multiple income streams leaves many individuals unprepared for financial success.

One of the most glaring omissions in traditional education is the lack of instruction on how money works in practice. Schools rarely teach how to make money work for you through investing, how to leverage compound interest, or how to manage risk through diversified investments. Without these crucial insights, many are left to figure out their finances through trial and error, often at a great personal cost.

How Traditional Education Focuses on Theoretical Knowledge, Not Real-World Financial Skills

Another major shortcoming of traditional education is its emphasis on theoretical knowledge rather than the practical skills needed to succeed in everyday life. While students may study the intricacies of economic systems or business models, they are seldom taught how to apply that knowledge in the context of their own personal finances.

For instance, while schools might offer courses on microeconomics or even business management, these subjects are typically taught from a theoretical perspective, focusing on abstract concepts and principles. They rarely touch on personal finance topics such as how to start investing with limited capital, how to manage cash flow as an entrepreneur, or how to minimize taxes legally. The curriculum often assumes that individuals will figure out these critical aspects of financial life on their own or through life experience, which can lead to costly mistakes.

This theoretical approach is especially problematic when students enter the workforce. The knowledge that could help them make better financial decisions—such as how to create a budget, invest in the stock market, or use credit responsibly—is absent from the standard curriculum. As a result, many people rely solely on salaries, unaware of how to grow their wealth through investing, real estate, or entrepreneurship.

Why Self-Directed Learning is Essential to Fill These Gaps

Given the limitations of traditional education, self-directed learning becomes essential for anyone aspiring to financial independence. Self-directed learning empowers individuals to seek out the knowledge that is most relevant to their financial goals, whether it's learning how to invest, understanding tax strategies, or exploring entrepreneurship. By focusing on real-world financial skills, self-education fills the gaps left by the traditional education system.

In areas like investing, taxes, entrepreneurship, and wealth management, self-education can be transformative. Here's why:

- **Investing:** Traditional education rarely teaches individuals how to invest in the stock market, real estate, or other vehicles. Self-directed learning provides the opportunity to explore different investment strategies, from value investing to growth stocks, and learn how to generate passive income.

- **Taxes:** Taxes can be a significant barrier to wealth creation, but traditional schooling doesn't teach tax optimization strategies. Self-education in tax laws and regulations can help individuals reduce their tax burden legally and keep more of their hard-earned money.

- **Entrepreneurship:** Schools often emphasize job security and working for others rather than starting a business. Self-education allows individuals to explore entrepreneurship, including how to launch a startup, scale a business, and navigate the challenges of self-employment.

- **Wealth Management:** Managing wealth requires a set of skills that are rarely taught in formal education. Self-education provides the tools to learn how to diversify income streams, protect assets, and create a financial plan that leads to long-term financial security.

3. Key Areas of Financial Literacy for Self-Education

Achieving financial success is not merely about earning more; it's about managing and growing your money effectively. Self-education in financial literacy provides the knowledge and tools necessary to build wealth, protect assets, and achieve financial independence. In this section, we will explore the five key areas where self-education can have the most impact: Budgeting and Saving, Debt Management, Investing Basics, Real Estate Investment, and Tax Optimization.

Budgeting and Saving: Understanding Personal Cash Flow, Cutting Unnecessary Expenses, and Saving for Future Goals

The foundation of financial literacy starts with understanding personal cash flow—how much money comes in versus how much goes out. Budgeting is the process of organizing and controlling this flow to ensure that your financial habits align with your goals.

- **Tracking Income and Expenses:** Effective budgeting begins with understanding where your money is coming from and where it's going. By tracking every expense, you can identify areas of overspending and unnecessary costs that can be reduced or eliminated.

- **Cutting Unnecessary Expenses:** Self-education in budgeting helps individuals learn to differentiate between needs and wants. Cutting out non-essential spending, such as frequent dining out or impulse purchases, allows for better allocation of resources toward savings or investments.

- **Setting Savings Goals:** Whether saving for an emergency fund, a down payment on a house, or long-term goals like retirement, budgeting plays a crucial role. A well-structured budget ensures that you can save a portion of your income consistently, preparing for both short-term needs and future goals.

By learning how to budget effectively, individuals can take control of their finances, reduce financial stress, and build a foundation for wealth accumulation.

Debt Management: Learning Strategies for Paying Off Debt Effectively, Avoiding High-Interest Loans, and Managing Credit

Debt can be a major obstacle to financial freedom, but with the right strategies, it can be managed and even leveraged wisely. Self-education in debt management focuses on understanding the types of debt, how to pay off high-interest loans, and how to use credit responsibly.

- **Paying Off Debt Effectively:** Not all debt is equal. Self-education teaches the difference between "good debt" (such as a mortgage) and "bad debt" (such as high-interest credit card debt). Effective debt management strategies, such as the snowball method (paying off the smallest debts first) or the avalanche method (paying off debts with the highest interest rates first), can significantly reduce financial strain.

- **Avoiding High-Interest Loans:** Understanding how interest works is key to avoiding predatory loans. Many people get trapped in cycles of debt by taking out loans with exorbitant interest rates. Self-education can help individuals identify red flags, compare loan options, and understand when it's best to avoid borrowing altogether.

- **Managing Credit:** A good credit score is essential for financial health. Self-education on credit management teaches how to use credit cards responsibly, pay bills on time, and maintain a healthy credit score, which can lead to better loan terms and lower interest rates in the future.

Debt, when managed well, can be a useful financial tool. However, when mishandled, it can spiral out of control. Self-education in debt management is essential for avoiding financial pitfalls and keeping debt in check.

Investing Basics: Learning About Stocks, Bonds, Mutual Funds, and ETFs. Understanding Risk Management and Portfolio Diversification

Investing is a key strategy for building wealth, but it requires knowledge and discipline to navigate successfully. Self-education in investing helps individuals understand the basic financial instruments and develop strategies for long-term financial growth.

- **Stocks, Bonds, Mutual Funds, and ETFs:** The first step in investing is understanding the available investment options. Stocks represent ownership in a company and offer higher returns but come with higher risk. Bonds are loans to companies or governments, offering lower risk and lower returns. Mutual funds pool money from multiple investors to buy a diversified portfolio of assets, while Exchange-Traded Funds (ETFs) offer similar benefits with greater flexibility. Self-education allows investors to determine which assets fit their risk tolerance and financial goals.

- **Risk Management:** One of the most important principles in investing is managing risk. This involves understanding your personal risk tolerance, the risk level of various assets, and how to balance potential rewards with the possibility of loss. Learning to avoid emotional decision-making during market fluctuations is critical to long-term investing success.

- **Portfolio Diversification:** A diversified portfolio reduces risk by spreading investments across different asset classes and industries. Self-education in diversification teaches investors how to allocate assets effectively to maximize returns while minimizing risk.

By learning the basics of investing, individuals can grow their wealth over time through compound returns and smart financial decisions.

Real Estate Investment: Basics of Real Estate as an Asset Class, How to Buy Properties, and Earn Rental Income

Real estate is one of the oldest and most reliable methods of wealth creation. However, many people are intimidated by the process of buying property or feel they lack the knowledge to invest in real estate effectively. Self-education in real estate can unlock this powerful asset class.

- **Real Estate as an Asset Class:** Real estate offers a tangible asset that appreciates over time and provides steady cash flow through rental income. Self-education can teach individuals how real estate fits into a diversified investment portfolio and the long-term benefits of property ownership.

- **Buying Properties:** Purchasing real estate requires knowledge of the market, financing options, and the buying process. Learning about mortgages, property evaluations, and legal considerations is essential for making smart real estate investments. Self-education can help potential investors navigate the complexities of property ownership, from finding the right location to negotiating deals.

- **Earning Rental Income:** Real estate can provide a steady stream of passive income. Self-education in property management, tenant relations, and rental market trends helps individuals maximize their rental income while minimizing headaches.

With the right knowledge, real estate can be an accessible and lucrative investment that builds long-term wealth.

Tax Optimization: Understanding Tax Laws, Deductions, and Credits to Keep More of Your Earnings

Taxes are often one of the biggest expenses individuals face, yet tax education is rarely provided in formal schooling. Self-education in tax optimization can significantly improve one's financial situation by teaching how to reduce the tax burden legally.

- **Understanding Tax Laws:** Self-education enables individuals to navigate the often-complex world of tax laws. Learning about tax brackets, tax rates, and how different forms of income (wages, investments, rental income) are taxed is critical for effective financial planning.

- **Deductions and Credits:** Tax deductions and credits can save individuals thousands of dollars each year. Self-education in this area helps individuals understand which deductions and credits they qualify for—whether it's related to home ownership, education expenses, or charitable contributions—and how to apply them to reduce their taxable income.

- **Keeping More of Your Earnings:** The ultimate goal of tax optimization is to keep more of what you earn. By learning about retirement accounts (like 401(k)s and IRAs), tax-advantaged investments, and strategies like tax-loss harvesting, individuals can minimize their tax liability and grow their wealth more efficiently.

By mastering tax optimization, individuals can legally reduce their tax burden, save money, and reinvest those savings to build wealth.

4. The Role of the Internet and Technology in Self-Education

The internet has revolutionized the way people access knowledge, particularly in the realm of financial literacy and investing. With vast amounts of information available at their fingertips, individuals no longer need to rely solely on traditional education to learn how to manage their finances and build wealth. In this section, we'll explore how the internet and technology have played a pivotal role in democratizing financial education, making it accessible to everyone, regardless of their background or location.

Access to Online Courses, Tutorials, Webinars, and Forums

One of the most significant advantages of the internet is the sheer volume of educational resources available on virtually any topic, including personal finance, investing, and wealth management. Individuals who are committed to self-education have access to a wide variety of learning formats, including online courses, video tutorials, webinars, and discussion forums that cater to different learning styles.

- **Online Courses:** Websites like Udemy, Coursera, and edX offer structured courses on financial literacy, investing, and wealth management, often taught by experienced professionals. These courses range from beginner-level introductions to advanced strategies for seasoned investors. The flexibility of online courses allows individuals to learn at their own pace and focus on the areas most relevant to their financial goals.

- **Video Tutorials and Webinars:** Platforms like YouTube and specialized financial websites host thousands of free video tutorials and webinars that cover topics such as budgeting, investing in the stock market, real estate strategies, and retirement planning. These resources provide in-depth, real-time learning from experts and practitioners, often offering step-by-step instructions on how to execute financial strategies.

- **Forums and Online Communities:** Discussion forums, such as Reddit's r/personalfinance or r/investing, offer a space for people to ask questions, share experiences, and learn from others who are on similar financial journeys. These online communities are valuable for self-education because they provide real-life examples and insights from a diverse group of people, helping learners understand different approaches to financial success.

Through these resources, the internet has eliminated many barriers to accessing high-quality financial education, allowing anyone with an internet connection to take control of their learning and financial future.

Platforms Like YouTube, Udemy, Coursera, and Blogs Offering Free or Affordable Financial Knowledge

A key aspect of the internet's role in self-education is the affordability of financial knowledge. Many of the platforms that offer financial education are either free or highly affordable, making them accessible to individuals from all income levels.

- **YouTube:** With millions of educational videos available, YouTube has become one of the most popular platforms for learning about personal finance and investing. Channels dedicated to financial education, such as Graham Stephan, Financial Education, and The Financial Diet, provide valuable insights on budgeting, saving, investing, and wealth-building strategies. These videos often break down complex financial concepts into simple, easy-to-understand terms, making financial education accessible to beginners.

- **Udemy and Coursera:** While some platforms offer paid courses, many provide discounts or free content for users who want to learn about finance and investing. Udemy offers low-cost courses on everything from stock market investing to personal finance management, while Coursera partners with universities to offer free or low-cost courses that grant certificates upon completion. These platforms cater to individuals who want structured learning experiences but don't want to commit to the cost or time associated with traditional higher education.

- **Blogs and Financial Websites:** Financial blogs such as *Mr. Money Mustache, The Simple Dollar,* and *NerdWallet* offer a wealth of free content on topics like frugal living, investment strategies, and tax optimization. These blogs provide detailed, actionable advice that empowers readers to take control of their finances. Often written by financial experts or individuals who have achieved financial independence themselves, these blogs offer a blend of personal experience and expert analysis that can be incredibly valuable for self-learners.

In short, the internet has democratized financial education by providing affordable and even free resources for people to improve their financial literacy. These platforms have created opportunities for individuals to gain knowledge and skills that were once limited to formal education or professional advisors.

The Democratization of Investing Through Tools Like Stock Trading Apps and Robo-Advisors

One of the most transformative developments in the financial world has been the rise of technology-driven platforms that make investing more accessible to the average person. Before the advent of online trading apps and robo-advisors, investing in the stock market was often viewed as complex, requiring expensive brokerage services and significant capital. Today, anyone can start investing with just a few dollars and a smartphone, thanks to these innovations.

- **Stock Trading Apps:** Apps like Robinhood, Webull, and E*TRADE have made it easier than ever for individuals to buy and sell stocks, ETFs, and other securities without needing a traditional broker. These platforms are user-friendly, often offering commission-free trades and educational resources to help new investors understand the basics of stock trading. This democratization of investing has empowered millions of people, particularly younger generations, to begin building wealth through the stock market with little upfront cost or expertise.

- **Robo-Advisors:** Platforms like Betterment, Wealthfront, and Acorns use algorithms to manage investment portfolios based on an individual's financial goals and risk tolerance. These robo-advisors automatically allocate investments across diversified portfolios of stocks and bonds, making it simple for people to invest without needing to have a deep understanding of financial markets. They also provide tools for tax optimization and retirement planning, making them an excellent option for individuals looking to grow their wealth over the long term.

- **Fractional Shares and Micro-Investing:** Another innovation that has lowered the barrier to entry for investing is the ability to purchase fractional shares. Apps like Stash and M1 Finance allow users to buy portions of high-priced stocks, making it possible to invest in companies like Amazon or Google with just a few dollars. This feature is particularly useful for individuals who are just starting their financial journey and don't have significant capital to invest.

The democratization of investing through these tools has opened up wealth-building opportunities to a much broader segment of the population. People who may have previously been excluded from the stock market due to high fees or a lack of knowledge can now start investing with ease, allowing them to take advantage of compound growth and build wealth over time.

5. Resources for Self-Education in Financial Literacy and Investing

Self-education in financial literacy and investing is easier than ever thanks to a wealth of accessible resources. Whether you prefer reading books, listening to podcasts, watching videos, engaging with online communities, or taking formal courses, there are countless options available to help you build the knowledge and skills needed to manage your finances effectively and grow wealth. Below are some of the top resources in each category that can guide your journey toward financial independence.

Books: Foundational Texts for Financial Literacy and Investing

Books remain one of the most effective and comprehensive ways to learn about financial literacy. They provide in-depth insights and are often written by seasoned experts or individuals who have successfully built wealth. Some of the most recommended books for financial education include:

- **Rich Dad Poor Dad by Robert Kiyosaki:** This classic book contrasts the financial philosophies of two father figures: one who believes in the traditional route of earning a salary and securing job stability, and the other who emphasizes the importance of financial education, investing, and entrepreneurship. Kiyosaki's key message is that formal education may not teach you how to manage money, but self-education can lead to financial freedom. The book introduces concepts such as assets and liabilities and explains why investing in income-generating assets is essential for building wealth.

- **The Intelligent Investor by Benjamin Graham:** Known as the bible of value investing, this book is an essential read for anyone serious about investing in the stock market. Benjamin Graham, a pioneer of modern investing strategies, introduces the principles of value investing, risk management, and long-term financial planning. The book teaches readers how to make smart investment decisions, avoid emotional investing, and maximize returns while minimizing risks.

- **Your Money or Your Life by Vicki Robin and Joe Dominguez:** This personal finance book provides a roadmap for achieving financial independence by transforming your relationship with money. Robin and Dominguez outline a nine-step program that encourages readers to track their spending, minimize expenses, and save more by prioritizing what truly matters in life. The book also promotes the idea of financial independence through simple living and strategic investing, making it an important resource for those looking to break free from consumerism and achieve financial freedom.

By studying these foundational books, individuals can develop a solid understanding of money management, investing, and wealth-building strategies that go beyond what is taught in traditional education systems.

Podcasts and YouTube Channels: Top Resources for Financial Education

Podcasts and YouTube channels offer a more accessible and digestible way to learn about financial literacy. These platforms provide valuable insights through discussions, interviews, and expert opinions. Here are some of the most popular financial podcasts and YouTube channels for self-education:

- **The Dave Ramsey Show (Podcast):** Dave Ramsey is a well-known personal finance expert who offers practical, no-nonsense advice on getting out of debt, saving, and building wealth. His podcast focuses on financial discipline and strategies to achieve financial independence, often highlighting the importance of living debt-free and following a step-by-step plan for financial success. Ramsey's approach is particularly useful for those struggling with debt and seeking a structured way to regain control over their finances.

- **The Money Guy Show (Podcast):** Brian Preston and Bo Hanson host this podcast, which offers a balanced approach to financial education. They cover a range of topics, including investing, retirement planning, tax strategies, and wealth-building. Their show combines practical tips with long-term financial planning advice, making it valuable for individuals at different stages of their financial journey.

- **Graham Stephan (YouTube):** Graham Stephan is a popular YouTuber known for his videos on personal finance, real estate investing, and entrepreneurship.

He shares practical advice on how to save, invest, and grow wealth, often using his own experiences in real estate and financial markets as examples. His content is accessible to beginners and covers a wide range of financial topics, making it an excellent resource for those looking to improve their financial literacy through engaging, easy-to-understand videos.

These podcasts and YouTube channels offer valuable financial advice in an engaging and interactive format, making them ideal for self-learners who prefer learning on the go or through multimedia.

Online Communities: Forums and Groups for Financial Independence

Online communities provide a space for individuals to share their experiences, ask questions, and learn from others who are also on the path to financial independence. These forums are valuable for self-education because they offer diverse perspectives and real-world examples of financial success. Some of the most popular online communities include:

- **Reddit's r/personalfinance:** This subreddit is one of the largest online communities dedicated to personal finance, with millions of members sharing advice on budgeting, saving, investing, debt management, and more. The community is welcoming to beginners and experts alike, making it a great place to ask questions, share experiences, and learn from others who have faced similar financial challenges.

- **FIRE Movement (Financial Independence, Retire Early):** The FIRE movement is a growing community of individuals focused on achieving financial independence and retiring early through disciplined saving, investing, and minimalism. Online communities dedicated to the FIRE movement, such as *r/FIRE* on Reddit and various FIRE blogs, provide actionable strategies for reducing expenses, maximizing savings, and growing wealth through smart investments. These communities offer a supportive environment for those looking to break free from the traditional work-for-life model and achieve financial freedom on their terms.

- **Investment Groups and Forums:** Online forums like *Bogleheads* (inspired by Vanguard founder John Bogle) and *The Motley Fool* offer a wealth of information on investing, particularly for those interested in low-cost index funds, ETFs, and long-term investment strategies. These communities provide in-depth discussions on market trends, portfolio diversification, and risk management, making them valuable for both new and experienced investors.

Engaging with these online communities can provide self-learners with insights, tips, and motivation from a diverse group of individuals who are on the same financial journey.

Courses: Overview of Online Courses from Platforms Like Udemy, Khan Academy, and Coursera Covering Financial Topics

For those who prefer structured learning, online courses provide a comprehensive and organized way to learn financial concepts. Platforms like Udemy, Khan Academy, and Coursera offer a wide range of financial literacy and investing courses that can help individuals build a strong foundation in money management.

- **Udemy:** Udemy offers thousands of affordable courses on personal finance, investing, and wealth management. Courses like *The Complete Personal Finance Course: Save, Protect, Make More* and *Investing in Stocks: The Complete Course* provide detailed, step-by-step instruction on essential financial topics, making it easy for learners to acquire the knowledge they need to achieve their financial goals.

- **Khan Academy:** Khan Academy provides free courses on a variety of financial topics, including personal finance, economics, and investing. Their Personal Finance section covers essential skills such as budgeting, managing credit, and understanding taxes. Khan Academy's courses are designed for learners of all levels and are a great starting point for those new to financial education.

- **Coursera:** Coursera partners with universities and financial institutions to offer high-quality courses on topics like investment management, financial markets, and retirement planning. Courses such as *Financial Markets* (taught by Yale professor Robert Shiller) and *Personal & Family Financial Planning* provide academic-level education on financial concepts and strategies, often for free or at a low cost.

These online courses offer a structured way to learn, with many providing certificates upon completion that can also be used to boost professional qualifications in finance.

In conclusion, the resources available for self-education in financial literacy and investing are extensive and diverse. From foundational books to engaging podcasts, interactive online communities, and structured courses, there are countless ways to build financial knowledge and skills. By leveraging these resources, individuals can take control of their financial future, develop a deeper understanding of money management, and achieve long-term wealth.

CHAPTER 11

PRACTICAL STEPS TO ESCAPE THE EDUCATION TRAP

Conducting a Personal Financial Health Check

Escaping the education trap requires more than just recognizing the shortcomings of traditional education; it involves taking concrete steps toward building a solid financial foundation. The first and most crucial step in this journey is conducting a personal financial health check. This process allows you to understand where you stand financially and identify the areas that need improvement. A financial health check provides clarity on your income, expenses, debts, and assets, and enables you to create a strategy to move toward financial freedom.

Step 1: Assessing Your Income and Expenses

The first step in conducting a personal financial health check is to assess your cash flow—how much money comes in and how much goes out. Most people have a general sense of their income, but many fail to track their expenses. This lack of awareness can lead to financial problems, as even small, seemingly insignificant expenses can add up over time. Here's how to approach this step:

1. **Calculate Your Total Income**: Include all sources of income, such as salary, side businesses, rental income, or investment returns. Knowing your total income gives you a clear idea of how much money you have available each month.

2. **Track Your Monthly Expenses**: List all your monthly expenses, both fixed (e.g., rent, utilities, insurance) and variable (e.g., groceries, entertainment, dining out). Use budgeting tools or apps to categorize and monitor your spending.

3. **Analyze Your Spending Habits**: Identify areas where you may be overspending. For instance, are you spending too much on non-essentials like dining out or subscriptions? Cutting back on discretionary spending can free up money for savings and investments.

4. **Calculate Your Savings Rate**: Once you have a clear picture of your income and expenses, calculate your savings rate. This is the percentage of your income that you are saving each month. A healthy savings rate is typically 15-20%, but aiming higher can accelerate your path to financial freedom.

Step 2: Reviewing Your Debts

Debt is one of the biggest barriers to financial freedom, and traditional education often fails to teach how to manage or eliminate debt effectively. In this step, you need to take an honest look at your debts:

1. **List All Outstanding Debts**: Include credit card balances, student loans, mortgages, car loans, and any other debts you owe. Make sure to include the interest rates and minimum monthly payments for each.

2. **Calculate Your Debt-to-Income Ratio**: This ratio compares your total monthly debt payments to your gross monthly income. It's a critical metric that lenders use to assess your creditworthiness, but it's also a helpful measure of financial health. A ratio of 36% or lower is generally considered good.

3. **Prioritize Debt Repayment**: To escape the education trap, you need to aggressively reduce high-interest debt. Focus on paying off credit card debt and other loans with high interest rates first. This strategy frees up cash flow for investing and saving.

4. **Consider Debt Consolidation or Refinancing**: If you have multiple debts, consolidating them into a lower-interest loan can make repayment easier and faster. Similarly, refinancing student loans or mortgages may lower your interest rate and save you money in the long term.

Step 3: Building an Emergency Fund

One of the most overlooked aspects of financial health is having an emergency fund. This fund acts as a safety net in case of unexpected expenses like medical emergencies, car repairs, or job loss.

1. **Set a Target Amount**: Financial experts recommend saving at least three to six months' worth of living

expenses in an easily accessible account. If you are in a stable job or have multiple income streams, you may aim for three months. If your income is less predictable, consider saving six months' worth or more.

2. **Start Small and Build Gradually**: If you don't have an emergency fund yet, start by saving a small amount each month. Automate your savings by setting up a direct transfer to a separate savings account.

3. **Keep Your Emergency Fund Separate**: Resist the temptation to dip into this fund for non-emergencies. Keep it in a separate savings account that you can easily access, but not so accessible that you're tempted to use it for everyday spending.

Step 4: Evaluating Your Investments

Once you've stabilized your income, managed your expenses, and started building your emergency fund, it's time to evaluate your investment strategy. Traditional education often neglects to teach the importance of investing, but it's essential for growing wealth and achieving financial independence.

1. **Review Your Investment Accounts**: Take stock of all your investment accounts, including retirement accounts (e.g., 401(k), IRA), brokerage accounts, and any other investment vehicles you use. Ensure you understand where your money is invested and how it's performing.

2. **Assess Your Risk Tolerance**: Your risk tolerance depends on your financial goals, age, and comfort with market fluctuations. Younger investors can typically afford to take on more risk since they have time to

recover from market downturns, while older investors may prefer a more conservative approach.

3. **Diversify Your Portfolio**: One of the key principles of investing is diversification—spreading your investments across different asset classes (stocks, bonds, real estate, etc.) to reduce risk. Make sure your portfolio is balanced and aligned with your risk tolerance and financial goals.

4. **Automate Your Investments**: Automating your investments ensures that you consistently contribute to your portfolio without having to think about it. Set up automatic contributions to your retirement accounts and brokerage accounts.

Step 5: Setting Financial Goals

Now that you have a clear understanding of your income, expenses, debts, and investments, the final step is to set specific financial goals. These goals will guide your actions and keep you motivated on your journey to financial freedom.

1. **Define Short-Term Goals**: These might include paying off a certain amount of debt, saving for a vacation, or building an emergency fund. Short-term goals are typically achievable within one to three years.

2. **Set Long-Term Goals**: Long-term goals could include saving for retirement, buying a home, or reaching a specific net worth. These goals often take five years or more to achieve.

3. **Create a Plan for Each Goal**: Break down each goal into actionable steps. For example, if your goal is to save $20,000 for a down payment on a home,

determine how much you need to save each month and how long it will take to reach your goal.

4. **Monitor and Adjust**: Regularly review your financial health and progress toward your goals. Life circumstances change, and so should your financial plan. Be flexible and adjust your strategy as needed to stay on track.

Conducting a personal financial health check is an essential first step in escaping the education trap and taking control of your financial future. It provides a clear picture of your current financial situation and serves as a foundation for making informed decisions. By assessing your income, managing your expenses, eliminating debt, building an emergency fund, and investing wisely, you can break free from the limitations of traditional education and move closer to financial independence. The road may not be easy, but with discipline, education, and a proactive approach, you can create the financial future you desire.

The Action Plan for Acquiring Financial Knowledge and Creating Wealth

Breaking free from the limitations of traditional education and taking control of your financial destiny requires a structured and actionable plan. This action plan outlines the key steps to acquire financial knowledge and build sustainable wealth. By following these steps, you can shift your mindset, gain essential financial skills, and create a long-term strategy for wealth creation.

Step 1: Educate Yourself in Financial Literacy

The foundation of creating wealth lies in financial literacy. Traditional education often neglects to teach key financial concepts like budgeting, investing, taxes, and debt management. To overcome this gap, you must take the initiative to educate yourself in these areas.

1. **Start with the Basics**: Begin by learning essential financial concepts such as:

    - Budgeting: How to manage your income and expenses.
    - Saving: The importance of saving for both short- and long-term goals.
    - Debt Management: Understanding good vs. bad debt, and how to pay off high-interest debts.
    - Investing: Basic principles of investing, including risk and reward, compounding, and diversification.

2. **Read Books and Blogs**: There are countless resources available to expand your knowledge. Start by reading personal finance books like *Rich Dad Poor Dad* by Robert Kiyosaki, *The Millionaire Next Door* by Thomas J. Stanley, or *The Intelligent Investor* by Benjamin Graham. Financial blogs and websites like Investopedia or The Simple Dollar are also valuable.

3. **Follow Financial Experts**: Gain insights from financial experts who offer advice on wealth-building strategies. Follow their podcasts, YouTube channels, or newsletters. Key figures include Warren Buffett, Suze Orman, Ramit Sethi, and Dave Ramsey.

4. **Take Online Courses**: Platforms like Coursera, Udemy, and Khan Academy offer free or affordable

courses on personal finance, investing, and entrepreneurship. Consider enrolling in specific courses that align with your financial goals.

5. **Join Communities**: Engage with financial communities, whether online or in-person, where you can share ideas, ask questions, and learn from others who are on a similar financial journey.

Step 2: Create a Financial Roadmap

Once you've gained a foundational understanding of financial concepts, it's time to create a personal financial roadmap. This will serve as your long-term guide to building wealth and achieving financial freedom.

1. **Set Clear Financial Goals**: Define both short-term and long-term financial goals. Short-term goals might include building an emergency fund or paying off debt, while long-term goals could involve saving for retirement or purchasing property.
    - Be specific about the amounts you need, the time frame, and how you plan to achieve these goals.

2. **Assess Your Current Financial Situation**: Take stock of your current financial health. Review your income, expenses, savings, debts, and investments. This assessment helps identify gaps and areas where you need to improve or adjust your habits.

3. **Develop a Budget**: A budget is the cornerstone of a solid financial plan. Create a budget that prioritizes saving and investing, ensuring that you live within your means while still working toward your financial goals. Consider the 50/30/20 rule:

- 50% of income on needs.
- 30% on wants.
- 20% on savings and investments.

4. **Establish an Emergency Fund**: Before you can invest or build wealth, it's critical to have a financial safety net. Aim to save three to six months' worth of living expenses in an easily accessible account. This fund will protect you in case of job loss or unexpected expenses.

5. **Eliminate High-Interest Debt**: Debt, especially high-interest debt like credit card balances, can undermine your wealth-building efforts. Focus on eliminating debt as soon as possible by using strategies like the debt snowball (paying off smaller debts first) or the debt avalanche (tackling higher-interest debts first).

Step 3: Start Investing Early and Consistently

Investing is the most powerful way to build wealth over time. However, it's essential to start as early as possible to take advantage of compound interest, where your investments generate earnings that are reinvested to produce even more earnings.

1. **Choose the Right Investment Strategy**: Determine your risk tolerance and investment goals. Are you looking for long-term growth, passive income, or a combination of both? Key investment options include:
    - **Stocks**: Ownership in companies that can grow your wealth through capital appreciation and dividends.
    - **Bonds**: Fixed-income investments that provide regular interest payments.

- **Real Estate**: Physical property that can generate rental income and appreciate in value.
- **Index Funds and ETFs**: Low-cost, diversified investment options that track the performance of a market index.

2. **Maximize Tax-Advantaged Accounts**: Contribute to retirement accounts such as a 401(k) or IRA, which offer tax advantages that can significantly boost your savings over time. Many employers offer matching contributions, which is essentially free money toward your retirement.

3. **Automate Your Investments**: Set up automatic contributions to your investment accounts. This ensures you invest consistently, regardless of market conditions or personal circumstances. Automation removes the temptation to time the market or skip contributions.

4. **Diversify Your Portfolio**: Avoid putting all your eggs in one basket by spreading your investments across different asset classes. Diversification reduces risk and increases the potential for long-term growth.

5. **Reinvest Dividends**: If you invest in stocks or funds that pay dividends, reinvest those dividends to purchase more shares. This simple strategy accelerates the compounding effect and increases your wealth over time.

Step 4: Develop the Entrepreneurial and Investor Mindset

To truly escape the education trap and build lasting wealth, you need to shift from a consumer or employee mindset to that of an entrepreneur and investor. This shift involves taking calculated risks, seeking opportunities, and focusing on building multiple streams of income.

1. **Think Like an Entrepreneur**: Entrepreneurs focus on creating value, solving problems, and leveraging opportunities. Start by exploring ways to generate additional income streams:

    o **Side Businesses**: Identify a business idea or a side hustle that leverages your skills and interests. This could range from freelancing to e-commerce or offering a service-based business.

    o **Passive Income Opportunities**: Seek out ways to earn money passively, such as affiliate marketing, online courses, or royalties from creative work.

2. **Invest in Yourself**: Personal growth and self-education are key to success. Continually invest in improving your skills, expanding your network, and learning new strategies. Attend seminars, read books on entrepreneurship and investing, and stay current on market trends.

3. **Focus on Creating Wealth, Not Just Earning Money**: Many people focus on increasing their salary without thinking about building wealth. True wealth comes from owning assets that generate income, whether through real estate, businesses, or investments.

4. **Develop Patience and Discipline**: Wealth creation is a long-term process that requires patience and consistency. Avoid get-rich-quick schemes and focus on steady, incremental growth. Stay disciplined with

your budget, savings, and investments, even when faced with market volatility or financial setbacks.

Step 5: Build Multiple Income Streams

Relying on a single source of income, such as a salary, is risky and limits your wealth potential. Building multiple streams of income is essential for financial security and growth.

1. **Expand Your Skillset**: Diversify your abilities to open up more opportunities for income generation. For example, learn a new skill that complements your current job or explore industries where you can offer consulting or freelance services.

2. **Real Estate Income**: Real estate is a proven path to wealth creation. Consider investing in rental properties, house flipping, or REITs (Real Estate Investment Trusts) to generate passive income through property ownership.

3. **Start a Side Business**: Develop a business that can generate additional income streams. E-commerce, blogging, or providing professional services are excellent starting points. A side business can eventually grow into a full-time venture, allowing you to diversify away from your job.

4. **Dividend Income**: Invest in dividend-paying stocks that provide regular income in the form of dividends. Over time, as you reinvest these dividends, you can create a powerful income stream that complements your salary or other earnings.

5. **Digital Products and Content Creation**: The internet provides countless opportunities to create and sell digital products, such as online courses, e-books, and

software. Additionally, you can monetize a blog, YouTube channel, or podcast by building an audience and earning through advertising, sponsorships, and affiliate marketing.

Step 6: Stay Committed to Continuous Learning and Adaptation

The world of finance and wealth-building is constantly evolving. Staying informed and adaptable is key to long-term success.

1. **Regularly Review Your Financial Plan**: Every few months, review your budget, investments, and financial goals. Life circumstances change, and so do market conditions, so adjust your strategy as needed to stay on track.

2. **Stay Informed About Market Trends**: Follow economic news, industry reports, and financial blogs to stay updated on changes that could impact your investments. The more you know, the better you'll be at making informed decisions.

3. **Network with Like-Minded Individuals**: Surround yourself with people who share your financial goals and are committed to growth. Attend networking events, join online communities, or form a mastermind group with others who are building wealth.

4. **Stay Resilient During Financial Setbacks**: Every wealth-building journey will encounter setbacks—whether it's an economic downturn, job loss, or an investment that doesn't pan out. The key is to stay resilient, learn from mistakes, and continue moving forward.

This action plan for acquiring financial knowledge and creating wealth is designed to provide a structured approach to escaping the education trap and achieving financial freedom. By following these steps, you'll develop the knowledge, habits, and strategies needed to build lasting wealth and take control of your financial future. Remember, wealth-building is a marathon, not a sprint, and success comes to those who stay disciplined, patient, and committed to continuous learning.

CHAPTER 12

THE ROLE OF MINDSET IN SUSTAINING WEALTH

Prioritizing Long-Term Wealth Over Short-Term Gratification

Building wealth is only the first part of the journey. The more challenging aspect is sustaining it over the long term, which requires a shift in mindset—one that favors long-term wealth over short-term gratification. This shift is crucial because wealth is not merely about how much you earn but about how much you retain and grow. Many individuals, even those who attain financial success, fall into the trap of instant rewards, only to see their hard-earned wealth diminish over time. In this chapter, we will explore how adopting a long-term perspective is key to maintaining and expanding wealth, and why resisting the allure of immediate pleasures is essential for sustaining financial success.

The Human Psychology of Instant Gratification

At the core of the challenge is human psychology. We are wired to seek immediate rewards. Whether it's a new gadget, luxury vacation, or fancy car, the desire for instant gratification is deeply ingrained. This behavior is often reinforced by societal pressures that promote consumerism. Advertisements, social media, and even peer influence push the idea that spending on material pleasures equates to success and happiness. However, while these purchases may bring short-term satisfaction, they can often derail long-term financial goals.

Wealthy individuals who maintain their success recognize the importance of deferring gratification. They understand that the fleeting joy of a new purchase cannot compete with the long-term security and freedom that wealth provides. Delaying immediate desires in favor of future benefits is a skill that can be developed, and it forms the bedrock of financial discipline.

The Power of Compounding and Time

One of the primary reasons to prioritize long-term wealth over short-term pleasures is the power of compounding. Compounding, often described as the "eighth wonder of the world," allows money to grow exponentially over time. However, it requires patience. Those who succumb to the temptation of spending their wealth instead of investing it fail to take full advantage of compounding's magic.

Consider an individual who invests a significant portion of their earnings instead of spending it on luxuries. Over time, the returns on these investments begin to generate returns of their own, creating a snowball effect. The key here is time. The earlier you begin investing, and the longer you allow your investments to grow, the greater the potential for wealth accumulation. On the contrary, frequent withdrawals or excessive spending on non-essential items cut short this process, stifling financial growth.

Shifting From a Consumer to an Investor Mentality

The consumer mindset focuses on spending; the investor mindset focuses on growth. To sustain wealth, one must embrace the latter. This shift means evaluating every purchase or financial decision not just by its immediate gratification but by its potential long-term impact. The wealthy are often characterized by their ability to distinguish between assets—things that will grow in value—and liabilities—things that will diminish in value over time.

While it is natural to want to enjoy the fruits of your labor, sustaining wealth requires a careful balance between enjoying life and securing your financial future. This is why many wealthy individuals live below their means. They prioritize investing in assets like stocks, real estate, and businesses that generate income, while keeping discretionary spending in check. In essence, they view money not as something to be spent but as a tool to create more wealth.

The Influence of Social and Cultural Factors

One of the biggest challenges in maintaining a long-term wealth-building mindset is the influence of social and cultural norms. In many societies, success is measured by visible displays of wealth—expensive cars, large homes, designer clothing, and luxury vacations. These pressures can push even the most financially disciplined individuals into overspending.

However, true financial success is rarely visible. Many wealthy individuals live modestly, investing their money rather than flaunting it. Sustaining wealth requires the courage to go against the grain, to resist societal expectations, and to stay focused on long-term goals. It's important to remember that those who indulge in short-term luxuries at the expense of their financial future often find themselves struggling later in life, while those who prioritize long-term growth enjoy financial freedom for years to come.

The Role of Financial Education and Self-Discipline

Maintaining wealth is not just about having money; it's about knowing how to manage it effectively. Financial education plays a critical role in sustaining wealth over the long term. Wealthy individuals continuously educate themselves about investing, tax strategies, risk management, and new opportunities in the financial markets. They understand that building and preserving wealth is a lifelong learning process.

Equally important is self-discipline. The ability to resist impulsive spending and stay committed to financial goals requires a high degree of self-control. This discipline allows wealthy individuals to continue making smart financial decisions, even when faced with temptations to spend or take on unnecessary debt.

Building Wealth That Lasts Generations

Sustaining wealth is not just about securing financial freedom for yourself; it's about creating a legacy. Many wealthy individuals aim to build generational wealth—money that can support not only their children but future generations as well. Achieving this goal requires a long-term perspective and careful planning.

This includes establishing trusts, setting up estate plans, and teaching future generations about the importance of financial responsibility. Without the right mindset, wealth can be squandered in just one generation. A famous saying goes, "Shirtsleeves to shirtsleeves in three generations," meaning that wealth is often built by one generation, enjoyed by the next, and lost by the third. To avoid this, families need to prioritize financial education and instill a long-term perspective in their children.

Conclusion: The Wealth Mindset

The key to sustaining wealth is a mindset that values long-term security over short-term pleasures. This mindset prioritizes financial growth, continuous learning, and disciplined spending. By embracing the principles of patience, compounding, and self-control, anyone can not only build but also sustain wealth over a lifetime.

True wealth is not just about the number of zeroes in your bank account; it's about the freedom to live life on your own terms, without the constant pressure of financial worry. To achieve this, you must make the shift from a consumer mentality to an investor mentality, always keeping your long-term goals in focus. By doing so, you will not only protect your wealth but also ensure that it continues to grow, providing security for both yourself and future generations.

The Ongoing Commitment to Financial Growth and Independence

Achieving financial growth and independence is not merely a one-time event; it's an ongoing commitment that requires continuous effort, education, and adaptability. In a world that is constantly changing—economically, technologically, and socially—maintaining and building upon your financial foundation requires a proactive mindset and a strategic approach. This section explores the key elements of this ongoing commitment, emphasizing the importance of lifelong learning, adaptability, discipline, and resilience in the pursuit of financial independence.

Lifelong Learning: The Foundation of Financial Growth

The financial landscape is ever-evolving, with new investment opportunities, technologies, and strategies emerging regularly. To stay ahead, individuals must commit to lifelong learning. This means actively seeking knowledge and staying informed about trends in personal finance, investing, and economic developments.

- **Read Widely**: Invest time in reading books, articles, and research papers related to finance and investing. Engaging with diverse perspectives can enhance your understanding and help you make informed decisions.

- **Attend Workshops and Seminars**: Participate in workshops, webinars, and seminars that focus on financial literacy and investment strategies. These events provide opportunities to learn from experts and network with like-minded individuals.

- **Utilize Online Resources**: Leverage online platforms and courses that offer educational resources on financial topics. Many reputable organizations provide free or low-cost courses on personal finance and investing.

- **Engage with Financial Advisors**: Establish a relationship with financial advisors who can provide tailored advice and insights into your financial situation. Regular check-ins can help you stay on track with your goals.

Adaptability: Responding to Change

In today's dynamic financial environment, adaptability is crucial. Economic shifts, market fluctuations, and unexpected life events can all impact your financial plans. To maintain growth and independence, you must be willing to adjust your strategies and approach as needed.

- **Assess Your Financial Goals**: Periodically review your financial goals and assess whether they remain relevant. Life changes—such as marriage, having children, or changing careers—may necessitate a reevaluation of your objectives.

- **Diversify Your Investments**: Diversification can help mitigate risks associated with market fluctuations. Explore various asset classes, such as stocks, bonds, real estate, and alternative investments, to build a resilient portfolio.

- **Embrace Technology**: Leverage technology to streamline your financial management. Utilize budgeting apps, investment platforms, and financial tracking tools to enhance your efficiency and decision-making.

- **Stay Informed About Economic Trends**: Keep an eye on economic indicators and market trends that may impact your financial situation. Understanding these trends can help you make informed decisions about your investments and savings strategies.

Discipline: The Path to Financial Independence

Discipline is a cornerstone of financial growth and independence. It involves sticking to your financial plan, resisting impulsive spending, and consistently saving and investing over time.

- **Create a Budget**: Develop a comprehensive budget that outlines your income, expenses, and savings goals. A well-structured budget serves as a roadmap to help you stay on track.

- **Set Up Automatic Savings**: Automate your savings and investments to ensure that you are consistently putting money toward your financial goals. By making savings a priority, you reduce the temptation to spend that money elsewhere.

- **Limit Discretionary Spending**: Be mindful of your spending habits, especially on non-essential items. Implement strategies to curb impulsive purchases, such as the "24-hour rule," where you wait a day before making significant purchases to determine if they are truly necessary.

- **Track Your Progress**: Regularly review your financial progress against your goals. Tracking your achievements can provide motivation and help you stay disciplined in your financial journey.

Resilience: Overcoming Setbacks

Financial independence is rarely a straight path. Setbacks and challenges are inevitable, whether due to market downturns, job loss, or unexpected expenses. Building resilience is essential to navigating these obstacles and maintaining your commitment to financial growth.

- **Embrace a Growth Mindset**: Approach challenges with a positive mindset. View setbacks as opportunities to learn and grow rather than as insurmountable barriers. A growth mindset fosters resilience and encourages you to seek solutions.

- **Develop an Emergency Fund**: An emergency fund acts as a financial safety net during tough times. Aim to save three to six months' worth of living expenses in a readily accessible account to cushion against unexpected financial shocks.

- **Reassess and Recalibrate**: In times of financial difficulty, reassess your financial strategies and goals. Adjust your plans as necessary, and be open to exploring alternative paths to recovery.

- **Stay Connected to Support Networks**: Surround yourself with supportive individuals who can provide encouragement and advice during challenging times. Sharing experiences and insights with others can help you navigate obstacles more effectively.

The Importance of Goal Setting

To maintain an ongoing commitment to financial growth and independence, establishing clear, achievable goals is essential. Goals provide direction and motivation, helping you focus your efforts and resources.

- **SMART Goals**: Use the SMART criteria (Specific, Measurable, Achievable, Relevant, Time-bound) to set financial goals. This framework ensures your goals are well-defined and attainable within a specific timeframe.

- **Break Down Goals**: Divide larger financial goals into smaller, manageable milestones. Achieving these smaller milestones can provide a sense of accomplishment and keep you motivated on your journey.

- **Celebrate Achievements**: Take time to celebrate your financial achievements, no matter how small. Acknowledging your progress reinforces positive behaviors and encourages continued commitment.

Conclusion: A Lifelong Journey

The ongoing commitment to financial growth and independence is a lifelong journey. It requires dedication, discipline, and adaptability. By prioritizing education, maintaining a disciplined approach to spending and saving, and embracing resilience in the face of setbacks, individuals can create a sustainable financial future.

This commitment is not solely about accumulating wealth; it's about gaining the freedom to live life on your own terms, pursue your passions, and provide for yourself and your loved ones. As you navigate the complexities of the financial landscape, remember that every step you take toward financial growth is a step toward greater independence and security.

Embrace the journey of continuous improvement in your financial habits, and let your ongoing commitment to financial growth be the catalyst for a fulfilling and secure life.

CHAPTER 13

THE FUTURE OF EDUCATION AND WEALTH CREATION

Introduction

As we navigate through the 21st century, the landscape of education is undergoing a significant transformation. The traditional education system, which has long focused on rote learning and standardized testing, is increasingly being challenged by the needs of a rapidly changing world. With the rise of technology, globalization, and an ever-evolving job market, there is a pressing need for education to adapt. This chapter explores the critical importance of incorporating financial literacy and entrepreneurship into modern education, arguing that these elements are essential for empowering individuals to create wealth and achieve financial independence.

The Changing Nature of Work

The job market today is vastly different from what it was a few decades ago. Automation, artificial intelligence, and digital platforms have disrupted traditional industries and created new ones. Many jobs that were once considered stable and secure are now at risk of being replaced by machines or outsourced to countries with lower labor costs. This shift underscores the importance of preparing students not just for jobs, but for a future where they can create their own opportunities.

The Need for Financial Literacy

Financial literacy is the ability to understand and effectively manage personal finances. Unfortunately, most educational institutions do not prioritize this vital skill, leaving students ill-prepared to navigate the complexities of financial decision-making. The consequences of this lack of education can be severe, leading to high levels of debt, poor investment choices, and an inability to save for the future.

To combat this issue, modern education must integrate financial literacy into the curriculum at all levels. This could include:

- **Basic Financial Concepts:** Teaching students about income, expenses, budgeting, saving, and investing.

- **Understanding Debt:** Providing insights into credit scores, loans, and the implications of debt on personal finances.

- **Investment Education:** Introducing concepts such as stocks, bonds, real estate, and the importance of diversifying investments.

By equipping students with these skills, we can empower them to make informed financial decisions that lead to wealth accumulation and financial independence.

The Importance of Entrepreneurship

In addition to financial literacy, entrepreneurship education is crucial for fostering innovation and resilience in today's economy. As traditional job security dwindles, the ability to create and manage a business has become increasingly valuable. Entrepreneurship education can teach students the skills necessary to identify opportunities, develop business plans, and understand the risks and rewards of starting a venture.

Key components of entrepreneurship education should include:

- **Creativity and Problem-Solving:** Encouraging students to think critically and develop innovative solutions to real-world problems.

- **Business Fundamentals:** Covering essential topics such as marketing, finance, operations, and management.

- **Practical Experience:** Providing opportunities for students to engage in real-life business projects or internships, allowing them to apply their knowledge in practical settings.

By fostering an entrepreneurial mindset, we can prepare students to thrive in an uncertain future, enabling them to create jobs rather than solely seek employment.

Integrating Financial Literacy and Entrepreneurship into Education

To effectively integrate financial literacy and entrepreneurship into modern education, several strategies can be employed:

1. **Curriculum Development:** Schools and educational institutions must collaborate with financial experts and entrepreneurs to develop relevant curricula that align with the needs of today's economy.

2. **Teacher Training:** Educators need specialized training to effectively teach financial literacy and entrepreneurship concepts. Professional development programs can equip teachers with the necessary skills and resources.

3. **Real-World Partnerships:** Establishing partnerships with local businesses, financial institutions, and entrepreneurs can provide students with valuable insights and experiences. Guest speakers, mentorship programs, and hands-on projects can enhance the learning experience.

4. **Technology Integration:** Leveraging technology can enhance financial literacy and entrepreneurship education. Online courses, simulations, and interactive tools can make learning engaging and accessible.

5. **Community Involvement:** Encouraging parents and community members to participate in financial literacy and entrepreneurship initiatives can create a supportive learning environment. Workshops and seminars can help reinforce the importance of these skills outside the classroom.

The Role of Policy Makers

Policymakers also play a crucial role in shaping the future of education and wealth creation. Governments should prioritize funding for programs that promote financial literacy and entrepreneurship education. Implementing national standards for financial literacy and entrepreneurship in school curricula can ensure that all students have access to these essential skills.

Additionally, policies that support small businesses and startups can create a more conducive environment for entrepreneurship. Providing resources, grants, and mentorship programs for aspiring entrepreneurs can help foster a culture of innovation and wealth creation.

Conclusion

The future of education must prioritize financial literacy and entrepreneurship as fundamental components of the curriculum. By equipping students with the knowledge and skills to manage their finances and create their own opportunities, we can empower a new generation to break free from the constraints of traditional education and achieve financial independence.

As we move forward, it is imperative that educators, policymakers, and communities work together to create a comprehensive educational framework that prepares individuals not only for the workforce but for a future of wealth creation and financial success. By doing so, we can transform the educational landscape and pave the way for a more prosperous and equitable society.

www.ingramcontent.com/pod-product-compliance
Lightning Source LLC
Chambersburg PA
CBHW071458220526
45472CB00003B/839